Herbert C McIlwaine

Martyrs of Empire

or Dinkinbar

Herbert C McIlwaine

Martyrs of Empire
or Dinkinbar

ISBN/EAN: 9783743306561

Manufactured in Europe, USA, Canada, Australia, Japa

Cover: Foto ©ninafisch / pixelio.de

Manufactured and distributed by brebook publishing software (www.brebook.com)

Herbert C McIlwaine

Martyrs of Empire

MARTYRS OF EMPIRE

OR

DINKINBAR

BY
HERBERT C. McILWAINE
AUTHOR OF "THE TWILIGHT REEF"

R. F. FENNO & COMPANY :   : 9 AND 11 EAST
SIXTEENTH STREET :   : NEW YORK CITY
ARCHIBALD CONSTABLE & CO., 2 WHITEHALL GARDENS, WESTMINSTER
1899

Contents

CHAPTER I

PAGE

THE BUSH FROM WITHOUT 1

CHAPTER II

THE BUSH FROM WITHIN 23

CHAPTER III

A HORSEMAN AND HIS HERD 42

CHAPTER IV

THE SPIRIT OF THE PIONEERS 66

CHAPTER V

GOING A-MILKING 81

CHAPTER VI

THE TYRANNY OF TRIFLES 100

CONTENTS

CHAPTER VII

	PAGE
SUNDAY ON DINKINBAR	111

CHAPTER VIII

| A BUCKJUMPING | 133 |

CHAPTER IX

| AFTERNOON TEA | 144 |

CHAPTER X

| SUSIE'S LETTER | 168 |

CHAPTER XI

| COLONIAL EXPERIENCE | 180 |

CHAPTER XII

| WHERE RACES MEET | 195 |

CHAPTER XIII

| IN TIME OF DROUGHT | 209 |

CONTENTS

CHAPTER XIV

	PAGE
God Sent His Messenger	219

CHAPTER XV

A Humble Remonstrance	228

CHAPTER XVI

A Day's Mustering	245

CHAPTER XVII

Martyrs of Empire	268

CHAPTER XVIII

At the Cross-Roads Again	289

CHAPTER I

The Bush from Without

A YOUNG man and a maiden sat facing one another across depleted breakfast things The girl had both elbows on the table, and the nails of one uplifted hand were idly busy about the palm of the other, also raised and spread out flat. The swift, squirrel-like, but totally unobjectionable little movements of the fingers gave evidence of a plentiful supply of that random energy of youth which in the less dainty leads occasionally to nail-biting—and worse. As she bent aside and forward and looked round her hands, there was a welcome in the eyes and a fervent curiosity in the parted lips and the three white teeth laid lightly on the under lip. Asked to describe her, women—most women—would have looked shrewdly at the knot of her hair and the set of her clothes and fastenings, and have cast about for a word that savoured of trimness and untidiness in equal mixture; men—all masculine men—would have seen the hands and face and ignored all else, and have said that she would lend grace inimitable to a flour-sack.

Men again, most men, would have said that the young man at whom she was gazing thus might be a good enough fellow if he would wear his hair shorter, do away with that studious disorder of silk necktie, and cease endeavouring to catch sight of his reflection in the black marble fireplace behind the girl's shoulder—and if that manly-looking touch of tan upon his face were not manifestly merely skin-deep. Women, on the other hand, unmarried or ill-married — these mostly—would likely enough have done as his sister was doing, and have regarded him with submissive adoration.

"Tell me, Jim, all about the place and what it's like; you came late last night, and I couldn't sleep for thinking of all you had to say. You have been away a year almost. And now during breakfast the mater has kept you on the proprieties and your health. You've been far, far away beyond all the tame things like cabs, and drapers' shops, and lectures, and all that?"

He tipped his cigarette ash delicately into the slop-basin with his right hand, folded the fingers of his left, and frowned judicially at his nails.

THE BUSH FROM WITHOUT

Then he looked at the ceiling, inhaled a mouthful of smoke, and sent it out thoughtfully and luxuriously in an upward blast. A pellet of bread his sister had aimed at a fly in the centre of the table struck him on the neck.

"It's a large order, Susie, and you're in the kind of hurry that drives a man dumb if he is any way careful about his phraseology," he said, looking at her.

She clenched her fist as women and other non-boxers do, with the thumb imprisoned, and thumped it three times smartly on the table, making the breakfast things jump. "Oh, bother your phraseology! Start at once."

"Where shall I begin?"

"At the beginning, and go on for weeks. Oh," she rolled her head distractedly, "pity the eaglet, or the pullet that thinks she's an eaglet, in the barnyard, hungry for the crags and the empyrean—that's rather fine, isn't it! But—what shall I say?—'The Song of the Open Road,' that's what's in me, and I want to know about the big, big world." She knit her hands, and planted them firmly in her lap. "What is it all like—the Australian Bush? Your letters amounted to just nothing at all."

He smiled indulgently. "Now you're talking; that narrows the question down to a single continent anyway. Oh," he said grandly, "yes. It's fine, and large, and free, and——"

Her fingers were busy again. She gave a deep-chested " Ah-h! And wild, Jim, with lots of daring."

His eyebrows implied a shrug. " Yes, and wild—oh yes. Not with the Red Indian, Fenimore Cooper wildness, perhaps, where the men never hoed their potato patches, or attended public worship, unless they had the trusty rifle within reach; that's over, so far as I could learn —what there was of it. But there's everlasting war with Nature to keep one's flocks and herds together, if not for the possession of one's scalp; and there's a fine primeval crudity about that."

" Yes. And that makes the people plain, and simple, and kind, and placid like their own cattle, eh? Of course there are no creeds, or fashions, or social problems, or competition, or—or intellectual maggots of any sort to set people disputing about what nobody can possibly know anything of. How splendid!" She had checked off the curses of enlightenment on her finger-tips, and now she spread out both hands towards him exultingly for his approval.

He fidgeted. "Look here, Susie. *Am* I starting, by special request, to give you my notions of the Bush after six months' sojourn in it; or am I laid on as a kind of stage chorus to endorse the conclusions of your inexperience with enthusiasm?"

She ran round the table, flung her arms about his neck and kissed him three times in different places, then took his cigarette and put it tenderly between his lips on the left, or wrong, side. "There!" she said coaxingly, putting her head against his, rocking him softly from side to side and patting his cheek; "it shall tell its story in its own pretty way, the pet. But I'm just that glad to see you back again, Jim dear. And I've had no one to hug while you were away—the mater doesn't encourage hugging. And I'm so hungry to hear about your adventures that I can't stop talking." She shook him by the shoulders and went back to her place.

He shifted his cigarette; her impulsiveness had rendered him more judicial, and he chose his words with even greater delicacy than before. "Well," he continued, "there's all that — that primordial crudity, if you like; and all manner of patriarchal simplicity—that is, if a man does the thing thoroughly. And"—he laughed, but not quite comfortably—"our excellent Uncle Joseph sees that everybody on his cattle-run is what he calls 'thorough,' or else quits."

"Ah, Uncle Joseph? I remember him when

he came over to marry Aunt Martha, as my first and only love. It was the mighty way he carried me on his shoulder and petted me in my tantrums. What is he like now?"

Jim's eyebrows lifted faintly. "Uncle Joseph is thorough, to his boots — even including them."

"Jim. You don't like him. Now, why; if he has lived this glorious, simple life?"

"I never said I didn't; and since the uncle and aunt are in London, having come home in the ship that brought me, and considering that you'll see them this afternoon, you must judge for yourself. Meantime, we are on the spaciousness and simplicity aforesaid. And you're under bond not to meddle with my way of telling my adventures, as you call them."

She knit her hands in her lap. "Go on, Jim, darling. But you don't like Uncle Joseph."

He blew another cloud thoughtfully towards the ceiling. "It's as spacious," he began, "as the ocean, and as simple as drinking tea, which they do in the Bush at every meal, and betweenwhiles. In fact, the similarity of the sea to the Bush, and the sailor to the Bushman, and life before the mast to the life of the normal Bushworker in the Never-never, or Back-blocks—by which is signified that territory not as yet wholly degraded by civilization—the similarity, I say, is striking."

"Oh, Jim, how clever——"

"Silence!" said Jim sternly. "I'm gathering the fruit of much thought and observation, and must be left uninterrupted. Very well. The sea is the sport and playground of the elements, so's the Bush; the sailor is the man what fights 'em, so's the Bushman. They're wide and wild, are the sea and the Bush; and wild are the men that go down to them in ships and on horseback. But then there's more to follow. Your sailor has Nature's choicest picture-book, as wide as the world, open at his elbow all the day and night; but he lives in a stinking fo'c'sle on food with the trail of the cockroaches over it all, that would ruin the digestion of anything but an ostrich or a burning fiery furnace. By night fleas, and worse, have him in their keeping; and rats, who indulge in hurdle-races over him, with his countenance for a take-off."

"Jim, Jim! Not in the Bush—it's hideous—"

"But true! In the Bush—in the Back-blocks, I mean—there's Nature at her weirdest and wildest right at your doorstep; cockroach-legs in your tea; maggots, as like as not, in your beef—if you get 'em once, which you're bound to, you live in horror ever after—and ants! Ants of every inconceivable variety, but chiefly black and iny, fanatically reckless of their lives, and simply of hellish industry in making themselves disagreeable. They send out skirmishers by the ten thousand, followed by millions in procession; and they're in and over everything, including your food and your blankets, and occasionally your ears. There's a variety of ant to make existence intolerable everywhere during each one of the twenty-four hours. Then flies, mosquitoes, spiders, scorpions, snakes in season, and innumerable sundries of a like order. The Bush is a Whiteley's emporium of maddening pests."

"O Jim, but this is awful! And can't you keep all these wild beasts in check somehow?"

"You can. A bus horse can pull his bus about for a couple of years, by which time he's due at the knacker's. I should say Bush people, Bush housewives more particularly, would not be long-lived—not if they're 'thorough,' and cursed with anything in the shape of nerves.

"Now, if I have made myself at all clear, so far," he went on with the contained enthusiasm of the lecturer, "I shall not have much difficulty in persuading you that when one's skin is on fire, and one's nerves are on the rack, owing to these seven-and-seventy plagues—not to mention that the food very soon turns what is left of one's digestion into a nightmare factory, working double tides—one's appreciation of the spaciousness, etc., is apt, to put it mildly, to get dulled. If you gave a man a stall for a crack play, for instance, on the one condition that he should attend the theatre with his under-things plentifully bestrewn with cow-itch, what sort of account do you suppose he would give of the acting?"

She smiled, but rather forlornly; the light had gone out of her gaiety, and her hands were lying idly in her lap. He apparently heeded only his own periods, which came the freer for her silence.

"A word more," he continued, "and there's the matter in a nutshell. With the sailor and the Bushman, the ever-present and inevitable is the cow-itch in his shirt—which is the insects and the raw, rude drudgery of his work, a never-ending war with Nature and all her pests. Now, the sailor or the Back-blocksman who goes through with that, and grows to look upon it as filling the bill of his desire for employment of his head and hands—why, he needs a nervous system of rope-yarn or raw-hide. And what sort of brain do you suppose there will be at the back of such nerves?"

She was picking dejectedly at the hem of the table-cloth, and said wearily and without raising her eyes, " You mean he's a brute, of course, and that the Bush after all is only a—a———"

" Is only, from the standpoint of even ordinary sensibility and intelligence, a physical, moral, and social swamp ? I deeply regret to say that I do. But be not cast down, sister mine. These are only generalities with which I felt constrained to lead off. At sea and in the Bush there's to be found occasionally such a person as the intelligent passenger and the enlightened visitor. That's me in both cases. I'm stored right to the muzzle with most entrancing detail and local colour, and characteristic turns of expression—most of 'em pretty strong—and stirring pictures from the wilds. There's rousing copy in it, Susie, when I can get at it."

" Copy," she repeated, absently, but doubtfully, " oh, copy. I suppose you people of the literary turn must find sermons in everything and copy in the Bush, even when you hate it—no, no ! let me finish !" and she held up her hand pleadingly before one of his superior shrugs and a tilting of his head that signified a hopelessness of the feminine understanding of questions in the large— " I don't understand these things, and we won't argue. But you've frightened me, Jim. If the Bush is such a piggy place and makes such brutes of men, what about poor old Ned being all these

THE BUSH FROM WITHOUT

years—it's seven now—under rough Uncle Joseph? You hardly mentioned him when you wrote."

"Ned? Oh! Well, Ned's grown broad and hard-handed; and he can do all that may become a Bushman, do it well—ride like a centaur, fell trees and bullocks, and—kill and skin and eat 'em too. Yes, Ned's becoming 'thorough.'"

She was watching him with a clouding face, "You mean he's grown big and brave, but wild and piggy. Jim, why didn't you bring him away?"

He laughed delightedly. "If you hunted the round world, I should say you couldn't light on a job to suit Ned better, unless you found something more wild and weird. Fancy him in any trade, profession or calling with pens and paper to it, and pews; or even in a place where bed-linen and roofs and carpets were considered as necessary to salvation from agonies of discomfort. Never no more for Ned."

Her eyes were full of tears. Jim was choosing another cigarette with great nicety. "Ned," he continued, as he felt among his pockets for a match, "is a beautiful study in degeneracy, and illustrates the pains and penalties that are attached to a sliding down the balusters, backways, towards the primevals, where our forefathers came from, instead of getting upstairs towards—well, the other thing, even if it isn't celestial. But there you are.

Some of us have got to grow beef and cabbages to make brains for the rest; only I don't take kindly to the hoe and the chopper myself. But Ned's built for it. And besides, there are Uncle Joseph's broad acres—or miles, as they reckon them out there—of land, and his herds, wanting an heir, and it struck me that Ned was about cut out for that honour, and that Uncle was disposed to smile upon his chances."

Susie looked at her folded fingers, and there was the faintest trembling along the line of her chin; but before either spoke again the door opened slowly, and Mrs. Thynne came in. She stood mildly wrinkling her smooth face at sight and smell of the smoke.

"Jim, *dear!* Smoking! And the breakfast things not cleared away." She looked feebly round the curtains, rang the bell, sat down on the sofa far away from her offspring, and eyed them in turn with an air of helpless protest.

Jim blew a series of rings before he answered. "I'm sorry, mater. It's colonial to smoke everywhere, and nearly always."

She nodded slowly, more in resignation than in acquiescence. "Very well, James; and I suppose your dear Uncle Joseph smokes?"

"Dear Uncle Joseph, if I'm any judge, smokes everywhere, even in bed."

THE BUSH FROM WITHOUT

"Jim," Mrs. Thynne said, appealing to her son's clemency, as if that were as near as she would venture to command, "you won't—you haven't quarrelled with Uncle Joseph? You'll show him respect, won't you, dear?" She smoothed her skirts complacently. "He's well off, and childless."

"My dear mater," said Jim, with extreme frankness and simplicity, "I have lived with dear Uncle Joseph for a year, and travelled with him for six weeks and more, and we are on the very politest terms, I assure you."

Mrs. Thynne sighed in relief. "That's a good son," she said.

Susie pushed back her chair and rose suddenly with the manner of one who remembers a forgotten errand. "I'm going out, mater. Oh, I shall be in heaps of time for lunch and Uncle Joseph," she added, foreseeing obstacles, and left the room.

She was ordinary enough, this young woman, in that she was ever ready to cast herself cheerfully upon the fitful current of her impulses; and only singular in that an obedient parent and an otherwise commodious environment left her free to do so to an extent not commonly enjoyed by the girl of even considerable advancement. So that, when Susie Thynne hurried on outdoor things by the help of only few and fleeting references to the mirror, and waited on the stairs for an opportunity that she might set out uncatechised, she had, in obeying the impulse of a moment ago, merely brought herself into a usual and congenial frame of mind. For her there was crisis in the air; but then the sense of impending crisis in their affairs is to many the necessary daily portion. She was flighty, there was no denying it, and ravenous of experience; one of those in whom, until the normal is accepted for better or for worse, intention still outruns the laggard purpose. She was ranked among her contemporaries as a kind of privileged vagrant, a gipsy among workers; at times—for she had her moods of intensity and gloom—a martyr without a cause. No plodder herself, she was the darling of sundry undistinguished plodders in every lighter line of feminine activity, from type-writing to tale-writing, and from the re-touching of negatives to portrait-painting. Something of a hare among tortoises, she saw the end while her fellows toiled upon the way to it; she would go a stage with them, putting new vigour into their stride, but finding the road too dull, the pace too slow, and the end unworthy, for herself—in other words, and in brutal truth, she had put her hand to many things and had grown tired of them.

THE BUSH FROM WITHOUT

Of a mixed ancestry, conflicting schemes were perpetually being urged upon her from the council-chamber of her faculties, prompting high purpose, but paralysing achievement. Thus she was uncentred, and as quick and complex as you please; or she was merely a girl of two-and-twenty, more frank-faced, perhaps, than pretty, such as you could match in London several hundred thousand times over, craving impossible breadth among life's littlenesses, and a cause amongst causeless hindrances; staunchly fickle, tempestuously steadfast; going with a bright colour and a free step from an arid West Central London square to the First Avenue Hotel. There she meant to see this Uncle Joseph with all his bourgeois after-breakfast crudeness heavy on him, before he should put on the armour of his company-manners—the very name of "Squatter," the grubbiness of it, made company-manners a dreadful certainty. She meant to figure in the interview as the calm-browed lady with the sword and scales and bandaged eyes, and to judge whether this rough old man did indeed appear to have had his heel upon the neck of her curly-haired, merry, sulky, splendid old playmate, Ned, grinding him into the mire of dull ill-manners, and a blighting solitude, and—and—*pigginess*—for that really summed up everything.

Here was a cause; here was a bend in life's road that would round into broader landscape at last, instead of the mud-walled, drab-hued, dusty highroad of her daily living. She was ready to do and dare all, so Ned were brought again amongst the things that were worthy of him. In truth, Uncle Joseph was prejudged. For Jim—shrewd, just, brilliant Jim—she adored. Jim had been to Cambridge, and had written in newspapers, and meant to write in books; and on such things as shades of character and men and matters in the rough could Jim act or think unworthily? Oh, no.

Yes, the gentleman was in his private sitting-room; would she come up? She went, proudly, calmly as she fancied, passing in appropriate review as she went the little she had learned of Saint Theresa, until a door was opened in some high, secluded passage-way, and she forgot Saint Theresa in the more imperative occupation of drawing breath without choking in a small room that was solid blue with cigar smoke—smoke that, nevertheless, she knew instinctively was from the burning of excellent tobacco-leaf.

A firm-knit man, nigh on six foot, was standing to receive her. The half-burned cigar was in his right hand, and the morning's paper hanging in a broad sheet; the fingers of his left were outspread

THE BUSH FROM WITHOUT

upon the table; he was gazing at her with his head shrewdly and kindly aslant, and with one eyebrow raised inquiringly, out of eyes entirely friendly.

"There," he said, with an unmistakable heartiness that killed all the harshness in his voice, though it certainly could not make it musical. "Come near the fire; sit down. Smoke bothers you? No wonder. Let's have some fresh air, or what they call fresh air in this place." He turned and eyed the window-fastenings doubtfully. "So you think you can undertake the work, Miss—Hines, isn't it?"

What there was of bashful maidenhood in Susie prayed that the floor might swallow her. There was some horrible mistake; if this indeed was Uncle Joseph, he took her for a laundress or something. At the same time that sure sense in her—the survival in nice women of the calm-eyed honesty of their childhood, had set the man upon his trial, and was giving her wildly contradictory reports of him. As for externals, his hands, scarred and furry, were the hands of a ploughman, and his weathered complexion that of a foremast hand; his clothes were roomy, and unmistakable reach-me-downs; his boots were bulbous and huge, with curves upon them like the curves of an upland fallow, and they fitted the feet as a nutshell fits a kernel. And yet, though manifestly he took her for a seamstress or such, he had stood to receive her, she was sure, not differently than he would have risen for a countess. Thus, while Uncle Joseph—if indeed it were he at all—fumbled about the window-sash, Susie held her crimson face with both hands and longed for extinction, and at the same time made these clear-eyed notes; winced at his skin and at his clothing, warmed to his true-ringing courtesy and his thought of her. It was the latter that drew her across to him in his strange helplessness at the window; she deftly undid the latch and opened it wide.

"These Chinese puzzles for window-fastenings are new since I was a boy," he said, still eyeing the sash; "and it's been more wood than glass in my windows this many a year, and pegs to fasten 'em. However, come and sit down, Miss— Miss—— ? "

"I'm Su—I'm Miss Thynne," she fluttered; "and, if you please, who are you? I mean——" It sounded like a nursery rhyme, she thought, and laughed distractedly.

"The Lord bless me! Not Susan's girl?" he said, taking off his spectacles.

"I should think she was," said a mellow woman's voice; "and why, Joe, you should deny

THE BUSH FROM WITHOUT

your own flesh and blood when it looks at you with your very own eyes, that beats me."

As she spoke, a fine, grey-haired woman came up to Susie, and with strong, kind fingers tenderly put away behind her ears some wandering strands of hair that had come loose through her exertion at the window.

Susie at the sound of the voice had turned in awe. Out of odd scraps of misinformation she had done for herself many fancy sketches wherein Aunt Martha took many shapes; but usually she was the unwomanly frontierswoman, short-kirtled and work-worn, with hard, curved hands, ready for any roughness, from milking a cow to drawing a trigger. But awe turned to reverence as she met two mother-wise grey eyes; and when she felt the caressing fingers upon her temples, she caught and kissed them, and put both arms about the grey-haired woman's neck. "It's my Aunt Martha," she said.

"Ay, it's Aunt Martha," the other said; "and surely God has sent you to me somehow for the wee thing I lost away out there. Look, Joe; it's what she would have been, the bonnie lamb."

Uncle Joseph had turned away to cough, and muttered that the poisonous London fog—although a breeze as pure as snow had rushed in at the open window—was in his eyes and throat.

But the women were crying unobtrusively together, and did not heed him.

Mrs. Thynne had for many years observed towards her children the attitude of a hen of extremely orthodox views who had been basely put to hatch out ducklings, and whose suspicions of something not quite normal about the tastes and anatomy of her brood since their emergence from the shell had received early and desperate confirmation by their putting forth delightedly and with unholy enterprise upon the bosom of the duck-pond. Stuart Thynne was an Irishman, and the inheritor of an estate which a sufficient number of ancestors had loyally exploited on the methods of the genuine Irish gentleman so as to bring it well within sight of insolvency. Not long after the time when the years brought on Stuart Thynne's turn to exercise the indiscretion of his fathers, something in him of cautious and foreign—his neighbours called it sordidness—set him figuring at his resources, with the result that he sold out and went to England. His action was hotly denounced by compatriots of the old conservative school, who, supported by their rotting peasantry, were booming serenely along to catastrophe. It was suggested that Thynne's desertion was traceable to a taint of Saxon integrity that had been intruded into the blood of his people about the time of the Rebellion. He braved the storm of indignation, however, and sold. Through no fault of his own—for he went into the market blindfold—he alighted on the crest of a swift and sudden rise in landed property, and, where he had looked for tens, got thousands of dirty English money for the ancestral bog-land and stone fences. He not unnaturally ascribed the gift of chance to what he called his Anglo-Picto-Celtic shrewdness, and on careful analysis of his character was astonished to discover that he was a born inventor with a turn for finance. He married a plain English housewife, one Susan Heyrick, to take firm hold of the good earth and to counterbalance the Irish top-hamper, as he said—for he had all his countrymen's facility and freedom in metaphor—and set his face towards industrial and financial enterprise. But he was too Irish. The Saxon strain was not enough to thicken and harden and weight the head; and in the balance of temperament that Irish heart would still outweigh it. It was the Anglo-Saxon in him that gave him his horror of debt and dirt, that led him to sell out of Ireland and to settle a sufficiency upon his wife; but it could not keep the results of his subsequent transactions on the right side of his ledger. His first considerable enterprise—the sale of his estate—remained his only successful one ; and it never occurred to him that that was not to be ascribed to his own acuteness. He lived long enough to beget the eager-witted boy and girl, and to see the various schemes in which he had embarked all his money founder irrevocably. His sound Saxon head was one day full of an invention that was to mend his failing fortunes, and his Irish heart was concerned for his baby-girl and her teething; and but for this preoccupation he might have had ime to save himself as well as the child that he rescued from beneath a runaway omnibus on Farringdon Road. As it was, he was killed. And it was a curious thing, hardly noted at the time, that at the inquest the bus-driver said he saw the gentleman's face below as the front wheel caught him, and that he looked glad ; also that he cried out in a very clear voice, something not in the English tongue.

CHAPTER II

The Bush from Within

SUSIE was placed between the uncle and aunt, and was aware, to her confusion, that she was unobtrusively worshipped by them both. It was worse than awkward, and humiliating somehow; and yet unspeakably grateful. Grateful, because Aunt Martha's adoring kisses, and the unerring tenderness of her hands, gave Susie the sense of bringing warmth and light to some part of the habitation of her being that had hitherto lain cold and unoccupied. It was awkward, because that something in her that had cried out in protest at first against these people and their rough ways would rise up to be reckoned with hereafter.

The manners of Uncle Joseph were, in a way, up to her nicest standards. And yet his boots and scarred hands, with their covering of bleached fur (though it was true his nails were trim and clean), and his bulgy clothes! Then his eyes;

behind that genial fatherliness was there not a leer, as of low commercial cunning? Was he kindly by the fireside, rude and a rogue in the market-place? And Aunt Martha? Even while that strong kind hand was at Susie's neck, and warming the cold places in her, a sense of guilt smote upon the girl as she winced at the clash of colour in her aunt's little antiquated cap that hid the lovely grey hair, and at the gaunt, grim cut of her clothes, of cheap strong stuff, coarse enough to set modern and metropolitan nerves ajar. As she contemplated Aunt Martha from the æsthetic standpoint, thorny thickets seemed to rise between them, and the heaven of their future relations grew black. And yet these two, to whom her heart went forth grudgingly, took her to their arms at sight, saw in her a worthy self she knew not. It was good to be hailed as of the blood and bone of these, the very offspring of sincerity. But in the vital, unessential matter of raiment! Susie held that every crease and crinkle every shade and texture in the clothing of man or woman, cried aloud of their wearer's character things that eyes and tongue were forbidden to utter; and she groaned within herself as her eyes roamed from Uncle Joseph's waistcoat and boots to Aunt Martha's gown and cap. Finally, she filled a pause in the conversation with a peal of

THE BUSH FROM WITHIN

laughter at the horror of confusion that had risen up within her.

Uncle Joseph wheeled upon her suddenly—almost scowling. But even Susie's laugh of distraction was very sweet, and his bushy brows lifted. "You reminded me then, though you're not a bit like him, of that brother of yours. I hope," he added elaborately, "he's very well?"

Susie set up her chin loyally. "He's very well, thank you, that brother of mine. Jim and I are so much alike, we might be twins."

"Ay, only you're not," Uncle Joseph said sternly, as if denying her entire statement. "Oh, your brother's all right, I dare say, for a Londoner."

"For a Londoner? And what am I? And what is there better than a good Londoner, Uncle Joseph?"

"Why, a man. You? You're fit for better things."

Susie thought the way he pounded his knee was almost vulgar, and turned to Aunt Martha, who was stroking her hand. "What does he mean, Aunt? Why doesn't he like Jim?"

"Joe, you're too sudden," Mrs. Heyrick said severely to her husband. "He has his hobbies, dear, about people roughing it, and the good it does them," she finished tenderly. But Susie felt, for all the fineness of the touch upon her hand, that she was left alone to champion Jim.

"Stand to your mates, girl, I like it," said Uncle Joseph squarely; "and you and me"—Susie shuddered slightly—"will be the faster friends for that. Your brother's very well, as I said, very well—um. And as for hobbies, if it's hobbies to put your cockered-up young fellows where they've got to show the stuff they're made of right through, then I'm chock full of hobbies."

"Jim is the best of good stuff then," Susie dashed in hotly, fronting uncle and aunt in turn as common enemies of her house. "He did well at college, and if he isn't clever enough for—the Bush"—she pulled up, aghast at the boldness of her own satire, but Uncle Joseph smiled encouragement, and rubbed his knees. She leaned towards him impulsively. "You *shall* like him, Uncle Joseph; if you like me, you must. He knows so much; you shall hear what they say of his writing. Aunt Martha, you know, we told you the wonderful way he took that scholarship."

"I know," Uncle Joseph said drily, "the way he took that steamship to get home to his ma. There, he's a regular ringer at his books, I don't doubt, and maybe an old bullock-puncher like me doesn't take enough stock in dictionaries and things." Susie shuddered at the antique illiterateness of the phraseology, and yet bubbled into a laugh, and loved the fatherly way her knee was touched.

"Now, there's Ned," said Uncle Joseph briskly; "you remember Ned?" and Aunt Martha echoed the name with the motherly vibration restored to her deep contralto.

"Ned? Remember dear old Ned?"—Susie's laugh was like a general handshaking—"jolly, sulky, clumsy old Ned. Tell me about him." She observed that a message in conjugal cipher passed between aunt and uncle; then Uncle Joseph rubbed his sandy beard joyously.

"Ay, I'll tell you," he said, looking deep among the coals. "I suppose he was just as big a fool and as much of a da—ha—hashed nuisance as the rest of the new chums, before I worked the green grass and the limejuice out of his constitution."

"Learn to talk English, Joe," Aunt Martha said, as the girl turned to her in perplexity. "It's the way the old hands talk about the boys fresh from home, Susie dear."

"When they're green and soppy, that's it," Uncle Joseph went on; "but I had hopes of Ned from the start. He used to make me talk forcibly, certainly, but he never wanted to put an umbrella in his swag."

"That's his blankets and things, when they go camping out," Aunt Martha interpreted.

"That's it; and I never caught him hanging boot-trees on his saddle to use in camp, or that kind of thing, that nearly all the new chums get up to. And when I stove in the hard round hat he arrived in, and gave it to the niggers, and burnt some of the tents and English rubbish he had got in the Strand here, and cut up his jackboots to nail on the brake-blocks of my buggy, and all that, he came round sooner than most of 'em to see I was right."

"He did, the brave boy," Aunt Martha said; "but do you remember the trouble there was, Joe, when he caught the cook going off with his nightshirts to make pudding-cloths of them?"

Uncle Joseph shouted with delight, but Susie put both hands to her face, which was burning. Aunt Martha pulled one of the hands away, and kissed the hot cheek. "I forgot, dearie," she said gently; "Ned told me you had made them. He'd have killed the cook, I believe, if he had torn one of them."

"And so on," said Uncle Joseph, having cleared his throat ferociously; "it was the same all round. He turned giddy when he saw his first bullock killed; but, Lord love me, three weeks afterwards there he was, blood to the elbows and the knife in his teeth, rummaging about the inside of the beast for a cut of the fillet for his supper."

"Joe—steady." The blood had ebbed from Susie's face as quickly as it had flowed there.

"Oho, well, he shut his teeth and he learned—that's all." Uncle Joseph rubbed his knee. "The day he got his first buster off a buckjumper—the black mare that nearly killed Count Moltke afterwards, Martha——"

Susie gasped. "Count——?"

"A blackboy, child." Aunt Martha was watching the girl's face like a Spartan mother.

"A nigger, certainly. And the mare trod on the calf of his leg, too—Ned's leg—as he fell, and missed his ear by the breadth of a sixpence with her hind foot. And what did he—Ned—do when he picked himself up? Well, he went dead white, and clung to the stockyard rail just a second; and he ground his teeth and caught the mare and rode her—ay, and she *could* buck—rode her till she stood and the sweat fell like rain off her—her——"

"Chest," Aunt Martha interposed firmly.

Susie breathed deep, and set her face to hear the rest. "And so he's getting on nicely?" she said formally.

"Well," said Uncle Joseph critically, "that's

a big word. I've put him right through the roughest road I could find, and that's fair to middling rough out there for a new-chum," he added grimly. "But Ned came through with it. And if he gets through the job I set him when I left without a smash up, you may take it—oh, yes"—with elaborate complacency—"you may take it, he's doing fairly well; *and*," with a chuckle, "he'll save his uncle about £100 in wages on the trip."

"And what is this job, this trip, Uncle Joseph?" Susie clung to her chair with one hand, and to Aunt Martha's wrist with the other. She was nerved to hear, almost, that Ned had been set to exterminate by scalping all his fellow-men within a fifty-mile radius of Uncle Joseph's homestead.

"It's just that he's on the road—or should be—with five hundred Dinkinbar bullocks, that's mine, to market; and the road's two thousand miles long, and there's some fall by the way, and—and the thieves spring up and choke 'em." Uncle Joseph drew up lamely amongst his mixed parables.

Susie laughed a sudden, rather tearful laugh at the breaking down of Uncle Joseph's imagery. "Two thousand miles? Oh, Aunt Martha! And he never wrote a word of all these troubles even when he did write, poor boy."

"Well," Uncle Joseph said heavily, " no, Ned's like me there, I'm afraid. Not much of a scholar, not like——"

"Joe, steady." Aunt Martha gave her word of command, and drew Susie to her. "Don't be frightened, my bonnie; we've lived among these things so long, and we can't but think you know what it's like. He makes it sound crueller than it is. And Ned's as strong and sound as a horse, and as true as a bell."

Uncle Joseph pursued his story with the convincing pertinacity of the tough-souled and the blunt-spoken that sets the sympathetic listener, unused to the lack of conversational tactics, upon the rack. Susie turned to him with no less fear than before, but with more show of fortitude.

"No, it's *not* so bad," he continued. "He's roughed it, has Ned. And if he fetches through to Melbourne with my bullocks—and he will, too—and makes a cheque for me, why, he may do more." He sat up in his chair and rattled the money in his pockets, nodding with lifted eyebrows. "Then he may run the station for me, and after me for himself, and some one else, who knows, hey? We're childless. That comes of showing grit, eh, Martha?" And again a message, unnoticed by Susie this time, passed between the eyes of the pair.

"And there's the hobby," Uncle Joseph went on dogmatically, "if you call it a hobby to take your young gentlemen of England and let 'em know what stuff they're made of."

Susie rallied to her cause. "By seeing whether they turn out good butchers, Uncle Joseph, and cattle-drovers, and get fond of messy things?"

He reached over and gave her shoulder a friendly shake that was to her at once a rebuke and a caress. "More than that, girl, a—a—devil of a lot more. If there wasn't soldiering, and the sea, and the Bush, and the likes of them to sort out the men from amongst us, and if it was all this cockered-up cuff-and-collar business you get in the towns, what would come o' the race?"

The sea again, and yoked to the Bush! Here were Jim's weapons in other hands; the sliding down the balusters of civility was being triumphantly vindicated. Susie was deeply persuaded that pernicious doctrines were being urged; but now the whole cause of enlightenment, as well as the good faith of Jim, were being thrust upon her to uphold, and she found herself unprepared for the task.

"No," Uncle Joseph continued, thumping his knee, and well set upon the business of unmasking the frauds called civilization and culture; "I've seen too much of it these thirty years to be taken

THE BUSH FROM WITHIN

in by your home-bred youngsters. Why, look at that last lot of new-chums that Snelling got out; wasn't that enough, eh, Martha?"

"The Honourable Mr. Snelling's a neighbour of ours, Susie," Aunt Martha explained; and added, nodding, "a very good neighbour. He's a brother of Lord Rainscourt's, you know."

Susie accepted this as a concession to her supposed home prejudices, and said vaguely, "Oh, yes."

"Oho, yes," said Uncle Joseph; "Snelling's a very good neighbour so long as he's watched close. But he taught me a thing or two about cheap new-chum labour," he chuckled. "When he came home to try and float his station and a lot of desert country at the back of it into a Company last year, and couldn't, he fetched out half a dozen new-chums as 'colonial experiencers' as the next best thing—got a whacking premium with each of 'em, of course. Well, I don't suppose you could have found a more mixed lot of what they call gentlemen's sons anywhere. Their fathers were all manner of respectable things, I believe, from a baronet to half-pay officers and doctors and things, and a big merchant. Snelling barred the retail trade because he couldn't knock a big enough premium out of them."

"All of them black sheep, of course," Susie remarked sweetly.

"That's just it, they weren't. Snelling barred that, too. He started in that line himself, and found it didn't pay. He——"

"Joe, steady," Aunt Martha called.

But Uncle Joseph was not to be quelled on this occasion, and his face darkened a little. "You know as well as I do, Martha, that the Honourable Snelling's as much of a swindler as he dares. No," he went on to Susie; "no black sheep. There were one or two of them had been slung, or spun, or whatever they call it, for the army, and by what they told me, if that makes a black sheep of a youngster, your flocks over here will do with a lot of thinning out. They were just an average sample. All well-spoken, clean-bred looking, upstanding youngsters, by and large as much alike as so many cockerels in a barnyard—at first. And they all brought the same kind of rubbish in the way of a 'colonial outfit'—all manner of artillery and bowie-knives and things they had got photographed in before they started. And of course," he added drily, "they were all ready to teach us old hands how to run our stations."

"Don't be too hard, Joe," said Aunt Martha, who was still watching Susie's face; "you know you said when you came away that two of them would turn out well; and he was a father to every one of them, Susie."

"Well, there you are—and I wonder who mothered the lot of 'em, Martha, eh? That's only thirty-three and a third per cent., and not one Ned amongst them. There you are; you see, girl?" he turned triumphantly to Susie. "Two went home again inside three months, funked it like—like anything. Two'll most likely die drunkards; and one of them took to moping and mooning instead of minding his business; and the Lord only knows how or where *he'll* finish—in a madhouse, I expect; and even of the two that look as if the tomfoolery might be knocked out of them, one's that dirty—Martha, d'you remember the day Odgers——?"

"I remember perfectly," Aunt Martha cut in severely, and shuddered.

"Still they're good stuff, two out of six, and it strikes me that's a liberal allowance, as newchums go. And there's your hobby. You leave those six at home, and they'd have gone through life just like the rest of these young Britishers, that nobody can tell one from the other, same as Chinamen, and they'd have married and settled down and been what's called a credit to their families, and have had pews in church, every one of them. But you take 'em and set 'em down out of the reach of all these things that keep them 'respectable,' and put their own lives in their own hands to do what they like with. Well, some of them haven't the heart of a chicken when there's nobody looking on; and some drink because there doesn't seem to be any disgrace to it; and they're nearly all as dirty as monkeys because there isn't a clean towel and scented soap always handy, and hot water brought up to their bedrooms. As for the moral side of them, they can't keep that two or three streets off and behind brick walls—there's a pane of glass let into them———"

Uncle Joseph had felt himself on doubtful ground here, and was consulting Aunt Martha with his eyes for instructions how to proceed, when a frizzed and pretty young woman was ushered into the room.

It was the typewriting young lady, by appointment with Mr. Heyrick, who received her precisely as he had welcomed Susie, whom, in fact, he had mistaken for her, owing to the bungling of the name. The new-comer showed some haughtiness—which, however, appeared to be entirely thrown away—at the familiarity of Uncle Joseph's reception of her.

While Mr. Heyrick was absorbed in a business

discussion with the young lady, Aunt Martha devoted herself to Susie as a mother might fall to comforting a child who had come without shrinking through her first visit to the dentist. Something stern, almost flinty, about Mrs. Heyrick—something that, while she was silently applauding her husband's hard conclusions, had seemed to match the unæsthetic cap and the rigid clothing—was now on a sudden laid aside like a suit of mail, leaving only the mild, submissive yearning that had first drawn Susie to her with the childish instinct that chooses its friends unerringly and instantly.

But very soon Uncle Joseph had bowed his visitor out, and came back rubbing and smacking his hands joyfully. And at once Susie was aware that the brief armistice was past; she prepared to take up arms again in defence of her own kind; she remembered Uncle Joseph's boots and his cunning smile, and Aunt Martha's discordant cap, and how the stuff gown had tickled her cheek.

"Oho," Uncle Joseph re-opened jubilantly, jerking his thumb towards the door, "this is a great institution, this type-writing. Snelling put me up to it. I'll get through all the business in a crack, and order this batch of new-chums in half the time, eh, Martha?"

"Remember you're not to take any I don't approve of, Joe," Aunt Martha said decisively.

"Of course not, old woman." He bent over Susie, and touched her under the chin very gently. "Your aunt's going to ear-mark my young gentlemen, and put the station brand on the boys' ribs herself, Susie."

Aunt Martha slapped the great paw and answered the girl's dumb, horrified inquiry—"It's more of his jokes, dear child; that's what they do with the cattle."

"But what boys?" Susie said, looking from aunt to uncle with her head high.

"Why," Uncle Joseph said triumphantly, "don't you see, girl, I'm going to teach 'colonial experience' to a small but very select party of young gentlemen, if I can catch 'em, at so much per head."

He sat down and chuckled, and the look that passed with Susie for greed and cunning was strong in his eyes.

"Going to make *men* of them, I suppose, Uncle Joseph?" she said.

"Ay," he returned heartily, mistaking her challenge. "Any of 'em that have the makings in 'em. If not, why, ho-ho, we'll send 'em back as returned empties, like—ahum."

"I'll take care of them, child," said Aunt

THE BUSH FROM WITHIN

Martha, almost apologetically, and stroking the girl's hand.

But Susie plucked it away; no less than a hemisphere lay now between her and the strong-faced woman, who, she remembered, was no blood relation of hers. But she thrust back her hand into Aunt Martha's immediately all the same, with the snuggling movement of a creature asking caressment. At the same time she said hotly to Uncle Joseph, "And they'll drink, and—and get—piggy, Uncle Joseph, and nobody to care, that's all."

"Ah, Sue," came sorrowfully from deep in Aunt Martha's breast.

"I didn't—I didn't mean it, Aunt Martha." Susie forgot the gown and cap again.

"Hey, Martha!" Uncle Joseph shouted, so fiercely and suddenly that Susie started and followed his eye to the fire in a dim fear of explosives hidden among the coals—"Martha!"

"Joe, steady," said Aunt Martha sternly; "you're enough to drive the girl crazy; you're not in the stockyard, remember. What is it?"

He turned to his wife with the light of news and a great discovery in his eyes, and pointing to Susie at the same time with three large fingers. "Martha, we'll take her with us, hey? She's the stuff—the real stuff. We'll take her. She'll see what Ned is; she'll see us straighten out these new-chums, and scrub the varnish off them. She'll believe us then. And maybe "—here he winked obtrusively at his wife—" maybe she'll stay." Then he plumped a hand on each knee, and squared his elbows, and looked at Susie as though all reasonable objection had been settled and done with.

There was a long pause. Susie looked straight before her; Uncle Joseph remained fixed, and stared forcibly at his niece; a deep, quiet sigh came from Aunt Martha, and she said at last very softly, in a tone that went straight to Susie's heart, "My sweetheart, if she only would! But there," she went on in a voice that was hard by comparison, "you're always sudden, Joe—and maybe you're fixed here. Susie, maybe the notion terrifies you," she added.

Susie was still looking wide-eyed into the fire. She shook her head slowly. "I'm not fixed," she said dreamily. " Plenty of people call me ' Feather-top.' No, I'm not frightened either." She saw nothing of a message of congratulation that passed between the eyes of her uncle and aunt.

"And there's your mother, child, would she——?" Aunt Martha paused and laid her left hand suddenly on her mouth, palm outwards, and looked hungrily above it at the girl.

THE BUSH FROM WITHIN

Susie nodded slowly to the fire, and said, still dreamily, "Poor mater, I think she would let me go." She smiled faintly.

The uncle and aunt quietly drew closer to the girl. "Then maybe—maybe, my lamb—you'll come with us," Aunt Martha said almost in a whisper.

The girl started as if out of sleep, and looked amazedly from one to other of the faces near her own. "I don't know—I don't know," she said distractedly, and, knitting her fingers close, she stood up and pushed back her chair, the two elder people following her beseechingly with their eyes.

"I must run," she said, and began to hunt feverishly round. Aunt Martha found her gloves on the floor; the other articles that Susie continued to seek hastily turned out, after all three had joined in the hunt, either to be in their right places or to have been left at home. Then she dashed into a precise description of how her mother's house was to be found, making uncle and aunt repeat the turnings and names of streets after her, and kissing them both lightly, she fled.

CHAPTER III

A Horseman and His Herd

SUSIE sped with a face of blind pre-occupation down the steps of the First Avenue Hotel, and was lost to the deferential gaze of the huge gold-rimmed door-keeper in the torrent of the Holborn traffic. She was still adrift and heedless of direction and of the surging vehicles round her, when she found that she had reached Holborn Circus, and that she was the object of much shouting, since the hub of a passing wheel was brushing against her skirts.

She saw as she stepped back upon the pavement that she had been menaced by a huge lumbering wagon, piled high with quaking carcases. It was groaning down towards the Smithfield meat-markets, whose pinnacles glittered cheerfully in the sunshine a little way to the left. As the wagon passed she looked up and met the eyes of the driver. He grinned when he saw her safe, then whipped his horse into a trot, and went whistling on his way. He was a great,

A HORSEMAN AND HIS HERD

gross creature, she observed, and his coarse blue blouse was stained with grease and caked with the blood of many dead, dissevered beasts. Susie watched him as he lurched whistling down the hill, and she continued to stand and gaze long after he and his grisly load had disappeared through a gaping portal in the markets.

It was given to that hulking wagoner to quell the riot in her thoughts, reducing them to most uncomfortable and convincing order. There, without doubt, into that charnel-house, went the embodiment of Uncle Joseph's ideal of what the man who had come to his full heritage of manhood ought to be.

To be a breeder, a tender, a slaughterer of beasts, a drover, a butcher with bloody hands; to be heavy-footed, heavy-jawed, earth-stained, beefy to the very soul—was that Uncle Joseph's ideal of manly fitness? Alack, it was. For how should it be otherwise? The very type of it had even now passed before her—had all but crushed the life out of her, and had laughed in her face; and Jim, her own brother and twin soul, had gone to see the finished product of manly living, and had found that it was as bad as the worst of her fears. All that there was in her of fineness and tenderness rose up in lament that her old playmate, the only unrelated boy-friend she had ever known, should have been given over to such a fate, and in revolt against the offering up of fresh victims in the form of Uncle Joseph's prospective new-chums. She turned towards home with a set face and a firm step. She would see what could be done to repair what evil had been already wrought, and to mend matters in the future. Here was a purpose high enough! It certainly appeared as if Crisis had overtaken her at last.

During those same hours, or thereabouts, when the season and the sun made it spring forenoon in England, and Susie turned back from Holborn Circus with the spirit of the martyrs awake in her, there was autumn and black night in Australia; near upon the time when the wagoner and his quaking load trundled downhill to Smithfield, and set Susie aflame with loathing of him and his tribe and trade, a drover, eight thousand miles or so beneath her feet, was on his way to market with beef.

He had been on watch an hour; it was three o'clock; at five there would show in the East that dim unshapen whiteness, the spirit of light that heads the pageantry of dawn. Shortly the Morning Star must send his steady radiance low down among the unmoving leaves. The drover

A HORSEMAN AND HIS HERD

sat with his hands crossed upon the pommel of his saddle, and faced to the eastward, watching for the star.

The cattle lay in a natural clearing of the open forest. Round about it, the ragged tree-tops ran in a broken ridge against the stars, and waste darkness lay among their limbs; but in the broad space there fell a spacious dimness like the last blink of twilight in a cathedral nave. Early in the night four great fires had been built, according to drovers' usage, to mark the cattle-camp; but these had been allowed to die down, and now where each had burned the embers sent out a crimson flush that showed great silhouettes of sleeping cattle and reddened the nearer tree-trunks. Faintly and far down the forest, a square blot of lesser darkness, the tent glimmered, and chiming now ever so faintly came the sound of the bells on the hobbled horses.

The drover had gone afoot many times round the mob, leading his horse and talking cattle-talk such as Bush beasts know well from infancy to signify man and horse, discipline and safety. Then he had mounted, for the watcher's instinct told him that there was about to pass that thrill of strange unrest that steals round the world in the waste of the early hours. As it goes by, every thing that sleeps is troubled, and all that wake are afraid, and the sick must listen for the beating of the wings of Death; it is the moment when cocks crow in the darkness with unseasonable clamour, and dogs howl as at the sight of some fearsome thing that passes by.

When that mysterious time draws on, the drover whose cattle are not yet wholly seasoned to surprises on the road must get a-horseback and feel his horse's bit and be ready, for the honour of his charge, and of his name and his blood—should his cattle rush—to ride and fear not.

A faint, distressful moaning spread about the camp; the drover turned his horse to face it, sent his feet hard home in the stirrup-irons, took a short grip of the reins, and started to ride slowly round. The mob had remained after their first lying down almost without stirring since their cud-chewing was finished; from the dim mass only big peaceful sounds of sleep had risen. Now and then one of the sentry bullocks would lie down, blow his vast breath of contentment, and another would rise to stand on guard. For set the purest farm-bred English cattle where alarms may come, and in a single day they will renounce the traditions of their centuries of safety, shelter, and refining, and resort to the warrior tactics of their long-horned, shaggy ancestors, and keep watch and watch against surprises.

A HORSEMAN AND HIS HERD

The moaning spread among the herd till the open space was full of mutterings and of a heavy stir, as beast after beast rose, stretched himself, and turned uneasily. Here and there one would lunge aimlessly with his horns at a neighbour, in a fretful drowsiness, then the neighbour would wake and rise to join the restless company, spreading unquiet in his turn.

Maybe a fourth of the mob was thus afoot. It was the blackest moment of the night, and with it the spirit of inquietude was passing westward round the globe. The drover called soothingly to his cattle; with half an eye he had seen, low down among the timber, the first white glitter of the Morning Star.

The dragging seconds of anxiety were nearly past; several deep-blown sighs had already told that the cattle were settling down again for their morning sleep. Suddenly from overhead there came the angry, tiny chattering of a possum, and a dead silence fell among the beasts; those that were about to settle stood. The snarling was followed by small sounds of furry combat, and then, as the loser was thrown out of the nest, by a rasping of claws scrambling for a hold among the strips of sere gum-bark—a noise that shook the stillness underneath like the sound of a trumpet; and at that, and with a great "h-rrr-mm" like

DINKINBAR

the grounding of twenty thousand rifle-butts on a hollow floor, every beast leapt up and stood. And the drover, as he raised a steady voice, could see, against the crimson ember-glow, the forest of upraised horns, the ears strained forward, the lines of the straight backs, and the arched tail-butts, all dead still as the beasts hung upon the brink of panic.

Another sound of scratching, harsher than the last, fell upon the bodeful silence, and a dry twig fell and snapped across the loins of a bullock that stood on the edge of the mob, facing the darkness and farthest from the man's comforting voice. That touch upon him meant, to his drawn, dull senses, that all the hidden horrors of the night were close upon him. He gave the high note of brutish terror, and laid himself out in a gallop to outrace his fears.

Before he had finished a single stride it seemed as if the whole dim multitude behind him turned from stone to flesh as the five hundred cattle streamed with an earth-shaking roar out of the open space and thundered down the forest.

The drover, and his horse as well as he, knew that wild note for the Bushman's call to battle. Even as the sound rose, the horse wheeled unbidden, and as he wheeled the drover set himself saddle-fast, rammed his hat firm, and gripped his

A HORSEMAN AND HIS HERD

hide chin-strap hard between his teeth. As the mob loosened itself to drive away in terror, the horse had already gained from the rear to the flank of it; before the beasts were well out of the open, he was hard upon their centre. But by then the bullocks had opened out for room, and were going naked, blind, and free as a flood, while the single horse that must head and stem the rush had his saddle and his master on him, had to mind the bit in his teeth, and skim wide of the rushing trees, since a touch of one of them was death to his rider. It settled down to a race—brain against brute, twelve stone of manhood and four sound hoofs against four thousand hundredweight of beef.

The rider's nerve and muscle were strained to their uttermost, but his mind was poised in a fine composure, keen and clear above the breathlessness of events like a well-handled surf-boat on the cap of a breaker. The grey-boled trees seemed to rise before him and rush by as if new-created from the chaos of darkness. The bark on one of them, where they were close set, snarled against his legging, and he laughed; nearer by an inch had meant a shattered knee, nearer by a foot, death, his horse going loose-reined and riderless. A low, straight limb showed up across his course, coming like a bludgeon aimed at his chest, if he should stay erect; he stooped forward in a leisurely way, and let it pass above him.

He found time to look across the torrent of heavy bodies that rushed at his elbow and to listen, as to the music of an orchestra, to the mighty ground-bass of the galloping cattle, and, through and above it, to the lighter sounds of desperate hurry—the tumultuous clicking of hoofs and horns like a very hurricane of castanets, the purr of the flying sand, and now and then a ripping and a splintering as sharp as the crash of cymbals, when the mob plunged through and scattered a patch of dead and brittle wood.

If ever the dead come back to watch us, then a great white company of silent horsemen, risen from the soil of many lands and out of many ages, rode through the night above the gum-tree tops, and looked down exultingly while the drover sent his blood-bay up from flank to centre and crept upon the leaders of his stampeding herd; if he and the blood-bay had ended the ride against one of those swinging tree-trunks, then, if ever the dead rise, the two would straightway have been called up to join the squadron overhead.

The drover said never a word till his saddle-girth was level with the horns of a leading bullock near him; then he uncoiled his nine-foot whip, and sent all there was of weight and will in his arm spinning down the throng till the cracker burst again and again about the eyes and muzzle of the beast, with the noise of pistol-shots and the sting of fifty dragoon-hornets in one. At the same time he wheeled his horse inward and set up the warwhoop of the cattle-yards. The bullock slowed in his speed and plunged aside before the noise and the fury of pain, the whip fell here and there like a rain of hot bullets, and the rout spread till the whole lead was turned. The horse moved as if to the drover's very thought, and, as the beasts came on crowding up to him, he worked his rawhide artillery right and left, till shortly the whole herd was surging about its own centre. A little more, and the drover's whip was coiled and on his thigh again, and he was talking the quiet cattle-talk and turning back the last weak rushes of the few beasts in which there still lingered the dregs of panic. The mob no longer whirled upon its own axis, but surged and simmered in many currents.

Presently, when they made to scatter, and when the drover heard peaceful sounds of browsing rise up from the dim herd, he knew the dangers of the night were done, and headed them towards a little opening in the timber.

The Morning Star had climbed beyond the tree-tops, and its cold, pure radiance shone like a jewel on the forehead of the dawn; down low, a pearly spread of light was putting out the lesser stars. It was already broad day, and there was a golden fume in the east, before one of the men rode out from the camp.

It was a bringing of beef to market, for weekly wages, even as when the blood-stained wagoner trundled his grisly load to Smithfield—only, down under there, the trails are longer, wider, freer somewhat than the sheltered, rutted English roads that the home-grown beef must travel from the pasture to the meat-block.

The man who turned away from the cattle to ride his two miles leisurely back to camp in the golden morning, amongst the long-drawn tree-shadows, had tasted the glory and the pride of good horsemanship. He went tacking forth and back, across and across the trampled belt where the stampeding bullocks had gouged the earth into innumerable hollows, and he sang loudly as he saw, alone in the smooth earth, clear of the fresh-torn cattle tracks, the steady, clear-cut line of his own horse's flying hoofs. This he followed back till it led him to the low limb that had threatened his life. He stopped his singing there, and rode slowly beneath the limb on his tracks, stooping low to let it pass above him; the bark brushed his shirt. He pulled the horse up, and, leaning a hand on the croup, turned and looked with round eyes at the rugged branch.

"If I hadn't stooped quite so far, Busyfoot, and if you hadn't been extended in a gallop, and consequently a couple of inches lower, maybe, than your proper measurement of fifteen two—what then, hey, old horse?

"What then, m-m?" He rode forward, stroking the horse's neck, his exultation past. "Le's see; five hundred of Mr. Joseph Heyrick's bullock's gone to scatteration; dust unto dust"—he looked at the arid ground—"mourning notepaper and envelopes for awhile, maybe. I fancy not."

He folded his hands on the pommel, and let the horse go loose-reined. "Uncle Joe? Jim Baxter?—hope they'd have given him my saddle —Aunt Martha?" He looked about him in a puzzled way.

"'Should the sturdy station children pull the bush
flowers on my grave,
I may chance to hear them romping overhead.'"

He looked round him again, shamefacedly this time, caught up the reins resolutely, but dropped them, and went on, scowling forward between the horse's ears. "No—no, child; Busyfoot, no wife, no—m-m?" On a sudden he melted, and began to whisper rapidly—"A widow, an unchurched widow there would be, Busyfoot; a black girl crying away up among the basalt ridges of Dinkinbar, crying like a dumb thing, the way they do. The way she did when I came away, and had to pull her arms from about me, and leave her lying there face down.

"'You go longa town now, Ne'die, big fella town. See um plenty white Mary,' she said; 'no more come back longa Noorna; no more, no more. Plenty kill umself me.'

"Did I say I'd come back? Heaven forgive me, I hardly know. But I do know she cried herself to sleep, holding one of my hands in both of hers. I mustn't. Never more. I'm going to town, Busyfoot, to wash the black stains out of me. God, they're bitten deep, though!"

There was the camp before him now, with its lumber of rolled swags and raffle of saddlery; the tent-pegs were sticking out forlornly, enclosing the flattened patch of earth and grass where the men's bodies had rested; a thin ribbon of smoke fluttered up from the dying camp-fire; a number of square-built horses, free or in hobbles or tied to saplings, stood round dejectedly, or strolled about nibbling absently at the grass-tufts. Three men, who were rolling up the camp-litter or saddling the horses, all dropped their work as Busyfoot's whinny to his mates struck their ears, and came out and stood in a row with arms akimbo to hear the story of the night's rush and the boss's ride to stop it.

He told his tale simply and peacefully as he sat cross-legged on a log and toiled reposefully with clasp-knife and teeth at the breakfast of beef and damper and a slab of cake that had been set apart for him, and washed the food down with long pulls at the dark-brown, much-sweetened tea. His audience, from the cook, who looked half pirate, half patriarch in his touzled greyness, to the younger of the stockmen with the face of a stolid wooden angel, hung upon his words, and made many eloquent listening pauses in their work of hoisting up the packs, and thumping the swags to tighten the surcingles finally about the pack-horses.

One of the men went back to join the cattle; the other forward with the cook and the loose horses to find and rig the night's camp; the drover in charge sat awhile on the log.

The place looked flat and desolate now in the broad forenoon sunshine, and was very still, save for a light droning of flies and occasional enquiring quawks from overhead, as the beady-eyed crows drew nearer among the trees and exchanged notes on the prospect of a harvest of scraps. There was a round impress in the ashes where last night's damper had been baked, a lump of rejected beef-fat was moistening in the growing warmth of the sun, and spreading a greasy stain about itself in the red earth; here and there a dried splash and a spurt of wizened tea-leaves marked where the men had flung out the dregs from their pannikins. The footmarks about the camp looked age-old already. The man on the log leaned an elbow on his knee and sunk his chin in the hollow of his hand; he held a stick in the other, and with it he drew scrawls on the sand between his feet.

A big, gentle sigh behind him stirred him to rise and turn. A stout, hairy-legged grey horse was hitched to a sapling—Busyfoot having gone free after his night's work; the grey's eyelids were lifting and lowering sleepily, and his head hung so that with the tightening of the reins the bit was dragging up his mouth into the semblance of a pulpy, fatuous smile. The man, as he noticed it, broke off in a gigantic stretch to laugh unreasonably; the horse raised his head and gazed lustrously at his master, pricking his ears and nickering with closed lips in a way that set his velvety nose shuddering.

The drover set his hat firm, and laid the chin-strap in its place, and rode off among the timber to join his cattle with the whip-handle set on his

A HORSEMAN AND HIS HERD

right thigh, the stockwhip in swinging loops, the grey going at a low-stepping steady walk. His back was scarcely turned upon the forsaken camp before six crows, their blue-black plumage shining like armour in the sun, swooped down and fell to strutting and quarrelling and clashing their iron beaks among the camp plunder.

The thick-set grey horse plodded patiently along for a mile or so, watching ahead amongst the lank, ash-coloured tree-stems for a sight of the moving cattle, his ears turning restlessly back and forth. The man, his body giving to the horse's stride with the firm unthinking ease that comes of living in the saddle, seemed, since leaving the camp, to have laid aside all memory of the tempest of action that had swept him through the strenuous dawning into the dull to-day, and to be as entirely re-absorbed in his dry routine as the horse beneath him. When the bright coats of the scattered mob showed up as they filtered slowly through the timber ahead, strolling and munching on their way, and sending up a peaceful hum like the sound of a distant factory, he took up his share in edging the beasts forward, flicking up the heels of the stragglers, and dodging in the flanks, but leaving it to the leaders to make their own sluggish pace, of a mile or so an hour, towards the night's camp, and thus onward daily to the trucking-yards at the railway terminus, fifteen weeks' journey to the southward.

There lay within the space of those few hours, between that stillest, blackest moment of the night before the first white breath of dawn was showing, and the broad forenoon sunlight, a fine epitome, in the truest setting, of all the trials and the duties that fall to the lot of the cattle-drover and the dweller in the back-blocks. The sleeping herd, the glare of the dying watch-fires, the ranks of sentinel trees, and the impenetrable darkness—then, out of the drawn silence, the stirring of all living things; the tremor of earth as the cattle sprang afoot, and the wild thunder of hoofs as they went crashing down the dark forest; the long chase with death unheeded threatening every stride; the winning to the front, the stormy, splendid wheeling of the living torrent, and its simmering and settling back to peace as the light broadened. And then, with the full coming of day, the sudden drop from the instant exercise of nerve and judgment, fit to head a cavalry charge or quell a revolt single-handed, to a daily, dusty, weeks'-long uninspiring mill-round of routine.

Utter solitude, for which men rave till they have tasted it, since to taste it leaves them dumb; for brief moments the kingly exaltation of fierce, free, headlong war against the brute forces of the

A HORSEMAN AND HIS HERD

world; to live in the main a life of flat drudgery, on which the simple body thrives, while the spirit, singly conservative among adaptive parts, hugs the traditions of home, and in revenge against the body's grossness stirs tender memories that ache and sting like a reproach—this is what the would-be frontiersman, whose wits are nimbler than his purpose is assured, must face, once the freer life lays hold upon him. The boundaries of our Empire are sentinelled by men within whom there goes on unceasingly this war between Old and New.

It was in the outskirts of a raw, rambling township far to the south that the drover yarded his cattle for the last time, and waited till the cattle-trucks were pushed gingerly down the railway siding to receive his mob, and roll it away for sale and slaughter.

Then began the final act of the trip in the crowding of the beasts into the funnel-shaped race and the ramming of them home into the open trucks that were pushed up one by one. The animals surged back at first from the mouth of the race and the open truck beyond as from the jaws of death, and then, driven by the hooting and prodding of the men behind them, crowded up and fought blindly forward.

The drover stood somewhat apart and watched

the packed and heaving crush, topped by the clashing horns, the straining eyeballs and snoring muzzles, and heard the hollow trampling on the wooden floors as load after load was completed, as if his pride in this triumphant ending to a long, successful journey were dashed with a sense of guilt that it was something of a betrayal of old friends into the hands of the executioner. As the work went forward, he hung farther and farther back. The cheerful comments of a row of local idlers roosting on the stockyard rails behind him, and the sustained and growing glee of his own men, whose blood was in a joyous simmer of anticipation of a spree in town, smote him with a dreariness that grew upon him as the numbers of the cattle thinned. The last truck-load was crowding towards the door, and at the tail of them all a noble, fine-horned bullock, his coat of white with its big, map-like, jagged splotches of ruby red shining with health—his certificate of clean ancestry and a temper as mild as his mother's milk—pulled up unconcernedly in the mouth of the race to give a rough-tongued licking to his ribs. As he finished his business of the toilet, the beast's eyes met those of the drover behind him, at whom he gazed long and meltingly.

"It's old Atlas," said one of the stockmen; "always in the tail. Here, hump yerself and yer

A HORSEMAN AND HIS HERD

joggraphy inter the meat-wagon," and he made to give the beast a final, friendly prod with his stick.

But the drover, stopping him, came up and rubbed the beast's quarter. Atlas strained his big eyes in clumsy gratitude.

"Damn me," the drover said quietly behind his shut teeth; "but I feel blood-guilty. You seem to be more of a chum this minute than the two-legged ones. Good-bye, mate; maybe we'll meet again." Atlas swung his tail slightly as if in salute, and strolled into the cattle-truck. He looked back without fear as he took his place, and the door was banged and fastened behind him.

"Must hev give them coves a heap of smart ridin' to fetch down a mob o' poddies [1] like that," a young fellow on the rail remarked cuttingly. He was in snowy moleskins and an ironed shirt, and had a crimson sash about his waist.

"Not the sort of riding, me son, that's done in townships, round the bar door, be flash men on quiet horses," a gentle, seasoned old hand said in

---

[1] "Poddy": a motherless calf, which, having been brought up, so to speak, by hand at the homestead, is distinguished in after life by his quietness of demeanour and total lack of fear, either of horse or of man. He gives, consequently, no excuse for brilliant horsemanship in the management of him.

a tired voice, leaning forward on the rail to fix the youngster mildly with his eye.

All the others in the roosting line regarded the youth with critical solemnity, and one said to him, "Chewed your ear, he did, that time, Charley." Charley muttered sulphurous prophecies as to what would happen in the next encounter.

On the strength of the support accorded him, the gentle old hand seemed to regard himself as deputed to convey the sense of the meeting to the drover and his men, who were now coming across the yard—the drover lagging, the men's faces filled with pride.

"I never," said the old hand, raising his thin voice, "I never see cattle better druv', mister, so help me Jimmy, and that's a big word, for I druv' cattle this thirty year; ay, from coast to coast, north and south, in the old days. Oh, don't tell me"—he raised his left hand, crooked at the knuckles, as if it always held the bridle-rein. "Show me a man a-yardin' and a-truckin' of his mob at the end of his trip, and I'll write him the character he deserves. It's the steady start, and none o' the hooray business"—he jerked a thumb towards the crimson sash—"and the man that never sleeps for the first month but what a whisper 'll wake him, and the pokin' and the pokin' along day in and day out as if a

A HORSEMAN AND HIS HERD

man didn't care if he grew old and died on the road, and was buried there between the tent and the cattle-camp. That's it, sir, that's *it*!" He pointed to the line of the closed-up trucks, and climbed soberly down.

The young drover faced the old one as he came to the ground, and straightened his back with an elderly shrug. The two exchanged a friendly look, and by tacit agreement moved away from the group at the rails, now growing noisy under the lead of the crimson sash.

"I'm not a-pilin' it on, young fellow," said the old man, returning to the matter next his heart, and kindling to a gentle enthusiasm; "but it isn't often I sees a drover these days as knows his trade, and likes it. When I does, I says so. Man, the drovers is a dyin' race. But them cattle of yours, mister, what with their coats and their condition, and the kind o' way they looked at you over their shoulders, familiar-like—well, there you are, there's your character wrote out big. And a good one, by Jimmy! And when a man 'll go up and handle a bullock like you done that red 'n white one—'Rattles' you called him?"

"Atlas. It was a joke of mine that the red splotches on him were like maps; and I taught a lad in the camp a lot of geography names off them, till the beast, always in the tail, 'd let me rub him down."

"There now, by Crumbs!" The old man followed the utterance of his mild expletive by looking the younger up and down with benign admiration, as a master craftsman might regard a promising junior. "And this Atlas wasn't even a poddy or a milker's calf, may be now, and a kinder pet to start with?"

"No. He was reared in the open."

"By Jimmy! Now there you are!"

"Never had a hair of him under cover till"— the young drover turned hastily, and shook a fist at the empty yards and the crowded trucks—"till I shoved him in that blasted wagon there. And now, it seemed a bit like going back on a mate somehow. — You'll call me a cow," he added hastily, aware that he had been betrayed by the old man's simple, whole-hearted admiration into an admission that would surely be misread.

It was not. The old man laid a hand on the other's shoulder. "See here now, have you wired your agents and got your papers fixed, and that? You have? Well then, by Jimmy, down you come with me to my camp on the river, and we has a feed and a pitch together. Lord save us now! but since I buried my old mate, Bill Summers, out on the Georgina, ten

A HORSEMAN AND HIS HERD

year ago, I haven't seen a man hardly that had the old stuff in him. Mates with your mob? Why, man, I'll be dinged, but there's been whiles that when I've been done a-truckin' of 'em I'd sneak off behind a tree and bite my knuckles for fear of crying like a woman, I felt that black-hearted. But these "—he rolled his head vaguely towards the yard with its roosting, gesticulating line, and the town, and his feelings seemed to outrun his words—" it's flash times, and hasty; come along down, lad; I have to say a lot to ye."

CHAPTER IV

The Spirit of the Pioneers

THE twilight was falling mellow and warm round the two men as they still talked restfully in the old drover's camp down in a secluded gully by the river, when into one of the lengthening pauses of the dialogue there fell the faint sound of clashing buffers and the scream of a locomotive in the town. The younger man rose hurriedly.

"I've got to shape," he said. "There's things to fix up for an early start in the morning—for town."

"For town?" The old man rubbed his knees slowly and stared among the embers of the fire; "for town? for Melbourne, eh?"

"Yes, for a bit of a spell, you know."

"Ah, a spell. Look there now, by Jimmy, but I'd forgot you was young and me old. To be sure, to be sure; there's the theaytres, and races, and the girls, and that. And you'll have friends among the squatter-folk. Ah." He ran faintly through the list as dealing with things of which he had long lost reckoning.

"Well, no," the younger man said, and the blankness of the elder seemed to have infected him somewhat; "I've no friends there. But I'll have a run round while I'm waiting for the boss and his wife to come out from England."

"Ah, well!"—the old man frankly relinquished his efforts after sympathy—"go, me lad, and luck go with you. I've been, and I tired of it. I'm happiest out of sight of the telegraph wire; and, by Crumbs, I'm nearer town this minute than suits me. You'll tire. You're the stuff they make the men of that's contenteder in the Bush. You're no rowdy, and none of these scholards that piles up the money-bags. Come back, and keep an eye out for me or me bones about the long cattle-roads somewhere."

They shook hands, and the young man tramped away with a determined air.

He went forward slowly in a slanting course up the shelving river bank, but stopped as the yellow lights of the town came into view beyond the silhouetted tree-trunks. Coarse and tiny sounds of roystering came over to him from the houses; he turned on his heel and sat down upon a felled tree-bole, facing the broad chasm of the river-bed. Above the still surface of the water-hole the giant eucalyptians leaned over their unflawed shadows, and these he watched till they faded, and till the reflection of a star laid open in the water beneath him an immeasurable gulf of silence.

It was late when he reached the town; few lights shone out of the straggling houses; but here and there along the wide, dim avenue of the main street the lamp-lit bars of the hotels still sent their splashes of light across the verandahs and out upon the bare roadway.

In the semi-darkness, close by one of these pathways of soiled radiance, a youth was leaning his forehead against his arm, thrown dejectedly across a verandah post; the whole figure drooped miserably. As the drover came near, he saw that it was his own lad, the youngest of the stockmen—the same who had learned geography from the hide of Atlas—and that the cook, who was seated on a bench against the wall, was delivering to the boy a drunken harangue. The old man was still half freebooter, half moralist; but the stimulus of intoxication had set the two forces disputing within him, like boys playing at "King o' the Castle," for possession of his thoughts and tongue; with the result that his exhortation touched in quick succession the extremes of ribaldry and devoutness. With one breath he would set forth in unstinted freedom of imagery the delirious joys that were purchasable in town for the hard-earned cheque of the Bush-worker; in the next he would come to the right-about and discourse with cold-drawn, puritan unctuousness, applying a wealth of sulphurous detail to prophecies of the wrath that was ready in the world to come for sinners against the moral laws of this life.

The note of supreme authority in the old man's voice died out of it when he heard orders to him to turn in sternly repeated several times in the drover's voice. He arose, weeping, and shuffled into an unlighted room, breathing softly to himself among his sobs a mixture of vague blasphemies and an inextricable tangle of references to graves, and sorrows, and grey hairs.

"What's the trouble, Matt?" the drover asked, as the cook's muttering died away.

"Who, me? Oh, *I'm* all right"; the lad rolled his head forlornly on his forearm.

"Come along down the road a bit;" and, when they stood alone, "Now then, sonny, there's nobody listening but me."

The boy set himself up defiantly. "What's the old —— want, then, slingin' his pitch about town, and his —— preachin', and me has to see them other two off in the morning by the train for Melbourne, mind you; and me has to start back—all that blinded way back—to the station with the horses. Oh no," with desperate composure, "*I'm* all right."

The drover paced quietly back and forth as the boy poured out his griefs. At one end of his walk he faced the line of the street, and could mark where the railway building topped the lower houses; at the other, the stars showed clear to the horizon. He stopped once in his patrol, facing towards where the road was swallowed at its outward end in the starlit plain. He took a mighty breath and returned to the lad.

"Never been in town, Matt?"

"Except you call this here sandy bug-walk a town. A was born under a bullock-wagon."

"Well, you might as well take a run down, now you're here."

"Eh?"

"You go along with Ned and Jerry in the morning, to Melbourne."

"To Mel—? And see the r—r—Races? Don't pull a cove's leg, boss."

"I'm not;' you shall go."

"G-a-w-d!" the boy breathed in awe; "an' see them crowds—and steamers—an' the sea!"

"Ay, the water-hole that wide it touches the blue sky. The whole lot."

THE SPIRIT OF THE PIONEERS

The boy's arms hung loose, and he stared stupidly at the man before him. " The horses ! " he shouted suddenly.

" I'll take 'em back. There's no grass here ; they must start right away."

The lad came nearer, and looked close into the drover's face with a suspicious shrewdness. "You'll take 'em back overland ? and you the boss ? and you won't go to Melbourne ? "

The drover shook his head. " Not this trip, anyway," he added. " I—I've business on the way up. I'm after—bulls—for the station." He caught the boy's arm and shook it. " Tell 'em that when they ask, Matt—bulls. See ? "

" I'll be damned ! " the boy said gently. " But I'll tell 'em." Then he shuffled, and began, in a flat sing-song, " I'm sure I'm very much obliged——"

" Think of the old man there, then, and don't go mucking round pubs, that's all. Kick up your heels every other way but that."

" So help me Christ ! " The lad held out a hand, and the man shook it. As they parted at the verandah, the lad stood a moment and watched the elder go away. " It licks me," he said to himself ; " the boss is a ringer, but——. Start back there ? — Do a four-month crawl away back to yon God-forgotten heap o' road metal they call

Dinkinbar Station?"—he jerked a thumb towards the Northern road—"and him might see the Races? Bulls be ———." And he sought his bed.

There is always a name wanting from the toast-list of the dinners that men eat in London when they gather together to count the gains and glorify the spread of our Colonial Empire. It is the name of the pioneer who goes out to the new lands, but does not return. It may be right that his name should be missing. It is not held seemly that a nation of shopkeepers should drink success to bankruptcy; a race of sportsmen does not toast the loser; the children and fathers of an Empire that is knit and armoured by the imperial cement of Mammon-worship—which is snobbery in the large—such men do not feel called upon to glorify the broken lives.

The stamp of unsuccess is set upon this pioneer; he is a bankrupt, he runs to lose, and is a failure. He is the unredeemed pledge of civilisation, the man before his time, the one who sows that his followers may reap. It is written that his forgotten bones shall serve to stake the boundaries of his people's territory.

He is the man who, single-handed, marks the line out into the waste lands along which is to

THE SPIRIT OF THE PIONEERS

follow later the baggage-train that bears the first blessings of civilisation—rum, rifles, commercial principles, religion, and the Flag, to hurry the heathen to a better world, that the white man, by the grace of God, may flourish in his stead. Under the hands of these second comers the idle acres wax fruitful where the pioneer has starved; and across the threshold of settlement, out into the wilderness, there lies the faint trail; and out there, twenty years' journey ahead for the bearers of the blessings of enlightenment, toils the pioneer, his face turned away from home.

So he moves on, the picket of an army that follows in his footsteps, yet knows him not. The solitude that he went out to subdue has absorbed him into itself instead, and he is a stranger to his people. Thus he does not come back to them; and that is how, when some of the men, who have helped to make our colonies, dine together in London, the name of the lost pioneer is not heard.

Shall we not toast him? Here's to him! Here's to them all! Comrades of the Great Lost Regiment, the one that goes before the flag, whose roster is unkept — the men who fight to lose, that we who follow them may win. Drink to it, Britons! Drink, all standing, to the Pioneers; but drink to the dregs, and then turn down the glass, in silence, for there is none to answer you.

DINKINBAR

When the young drover trucked the last of his mob in the railway yards and turned away, smitten with a vague loneliness and remorse, and yet with a horror of distaste upon him, too, for the roar and racket of a strange city, and when the mild voice of the old hand from the stockyard rail set at peace the jarring humours in him, it was the voice of the pioneer that called to him, out from the land of sundown.

The answering note to it that sang in him showed, unknown to himself, that the wilderness had set its mark upon him. The voice was pitched in the right key to remind him that out there was peace; the town ahead of him had become a populous desolation.

The same man, too, as he rode leisurely, many weeks later, with the setting sun on his left hand, towards the lonely Dinkinbar out-station, seemed to find his surroundings as soothing as his thoughts of the blare and bustle of a town had been distressful.

It was in that moment of time when the earth, having lain all day in a staring monotony of colour, kindles suddenly into a glory of tawny and purple-red and golden-green. The level valley of the sward tapered to a point where its flanking ridges met; and there, half hidden amongst the trees, the bark walls of the out-station glowed like plates of burnished copper. On the ridges, the lumps of naked basalt, the dull red earth, and the tussocks of half-sere grass all shone for the moment like heaped-up riches; even the black-holed, scant-leaved ironbarks flamed like huge exotics. Down the centre of the little valley, cleaving the greensward, ran a liquid ribbon of water between low banks, with the rich black soil, here and there invaded and concealed by curving brows of green sod, showing in miniature cliffs or in shelving beaches where the cattle came to drink. The water, clear-drawn and cold from its source among the black ranges, ran with a merry, noiseless bustle, and was gay upon its surface with a changing multitude of reflections.

The man drew rein and looked about him. Far back amongst the ranges there rose the strong, clear trumpeting of a bull; a flock of pink-breasted parrots swept past him with a silken rush of wings, whirled downward as if by word of command, settled and spread along the water, and chattered at their drinking. The yellow sunlight struck amongst the hair of the horse's neck in little mists of many-coloured fire. The whole arch of heaven was stainless. From a huge height above the western ridge, a hawk was wheeling downward in a mighty spiral. The horse stood like a statue, with ears pricked; then his chest filled and sank, making the leather cringe, and he plucked gently forward on the bit. The rider loosed up the reins and rode slowly on.

He was still two hundred yards from the hut, when he pulled up once more. The sunlight glory had died away from the earth more quickly than it had come; the face of the stream was already leaden. The horseman looked above him. A thin black thread was drawn across the blue; it was the telegraph wire, and away to west and east the posts that carried it stood stark and even in a row. Where their line crested the ridges, the forest timber that had been felled to make space for them lay bleaching about their feet like the bones of dead leviathans. The wire hummed its metallic note of sleepless hurry, and as the man listened and looked, the thin peace-devouring song plucked his thoughts from their twilight slumbrousness and sent them spinning abroad as swiftly as the invisible current overhead. Once before—how long ago was it since he had started on the droving trip?—it had sung to him its song of life, and he had stood to listen. Then his mind had run, as now, away down the track of the wire, down the long line of the naked posts—the line that strode the continent amongst the felled tree-trunks as down a hurricane-track—to the splendid turmoil of the town. His blood had thrilled to it; he had looked back guiltily, longingly, towards the unlighted hut, whence had come a sound of moaning; then he had spurred his horse to a gallop down the green flat, without looking behind him, as though, had he lingered, the moaning thing might have clung to him and held him from his own kind. And now, as he faced the out-station hut again and felt in his ears the restless song of the wire, a nameless dread laid hold of him, and the sweat started on his forehead. The city had cried out to him, and he had come; but when he had drawn near it, what was the dumb thing that had laid hold of him, bidding him turn back again? Why did the distance call?—where was the right? —whose was the wrong?

The horse pulled at the bit again, and struck the ground impatiently with a forefoot and whinnied lightly; the rider had sat still in the saddle till the twilight had crept about him, and the hut was already hidden amongst the trees. A pattering like the sound of naked feet sounded among the dry leaves about the hut, and stopped. The rider turned his horse from the sound and looked up at the wire, and remained looking upward while the footsteps sounded again, paused, and came on repeatedly, as if working towards him from tree to tree. The horseman sat still and closed his eyes, turning his face still towards the wire.

"What name you, white-fellow?" It was a croaking voice, and the words came from behind a tree not twenty yards away.

The horseman opened his eyes, but did not look round. "Who's there?" he called sharply.

"Mardie—o-o-old fella Mardie," croaked the voice; "you Nédie, mine thinkit."

"*Yo-ai* (yes), me, Nédie. Mardie, where's—which way stop that one daughter belong you—Noorna?"

A thin, piteous keening sounded from behind the tree. It was nearly dark now; the man fell to shaking in the saddle. "God forgive me," he whispered, "but it's the best." The crying stopped, and he repeated the question.

"That one little fella Noorna dead, plenty dead," wailed the voice—"stop longa ground. That one he say, 'Nédie go 'long, big fella town, no more come back, me die, me die, me die," and more wailing followed.

The horseman without a word faced slowly round the way he had come, and rode back along the flat with his head falling forward.

"Nédie, Nédie!" There was a running of light footsteps behind him, and a slim, dusky little shape clad in a single garment darted from behind the tree, flung itself down by the horse and clung with both hands to the rider's foot. The horse stopped of his own accord, and as at one of his own kind gazed round benevolently at the bowed figure.

The man looked down, breathing deep and slowly. " Noorna," he said dully, " Noorna."

She flung out both hands and threw back her head, looking up at him radiantly as she knelt. " Nédie, Nédie," she breathed rapturously, "you come back." Then she cowered again, and taking his foot in both hands she pressed it on her bowed head and shuddered like a frightened child. " Me Noorna, me no dead," she sobbed brokenly; "no Mardie—me mimicky that one—no angeree you? So glad, me—too glad, too glad. You come back." She moaned and laughed like a dumb thing.

He reached down and caught one of the round forearms, and she rose up slowly. He pulled gently on the arm and held out his foot; she placed one of hers upon it, and he raised her up before him on the saddle. He held her to him, and she snuggled close against him, still sobbing and crying by turns, as he wheeled the horse towards the hut again.

They were still a dozen paces short of it when the clink of horse-shoes along the stony track beyond it reached them faintly. The horseman lowered the girl softly, with a whispered caution to her to come when he called, and was taking off his saddle when a rider from the lonely telegraph repeating-station five miles away drew up at the hut.

The messenger, overjoyed at finding some one at the out-station when he had counted on a lonely night ride to the homestead, stayed till long after supper. All the time until he left he talked incessantly, showing the greediness of the man who is much alone for the sound of his own voice, recalling disjointed items of the world's news he had recently heard ticked out as they crossed the basalt ridge on their way to and from the ends of the earth, and furnishing a wild commentary upon them.

As the tramp of the messenger's horse died away at last among the stones, the drover leaned against the doorway of the hut with the message in his hand, and gazed for a long time down the dark ridge where, by the water at its foot, the fire at the blacks' camp glowed sullenly. A subdued muttering of voices rose from about the light.

"My Uncle Joseph will be at the head station to-morrow night, and his chummies a day later," he said blankly, as if the words, owing to many repetitions, had lost their meaning. "Oy, Noorna!" he called, and the light footsteps came flying towards him from the fire.

CHAPTER V

Going a-Milking

THE horseman started late on his lonely ten-mile ride to the homestead next day, and loitered much by the way, making many fruitless detours to right and left of the track amongst distant mobs of cattle, at which he gazed long and absently. It was already long after dark when he fell in with six cows and calves, and, smitten apparently with a sudden energy, set himself to drive them to the station. Under the lead of the oldest cow, the little mob displayed that refinement of aggravation—that brute rebellion against common sense that has much in it of the seeming malevolence of inanimate things—which has soured and broken more spirits and tempers in the Bush than bad whiskey has ever done. The cattle would do everything but keep the road, and they infected the man behind them with their blind obstinacy. It was midnight when he yarded them, and by then he, his dog, and his horse were dazed and drunken with fatigue.

As he swung to the last heavy stockyard gate

and pegged it, the peace that comes to tired men settled down upon him. He leaned his forehead for a moment on a rail, folded his arms upon the next, and watched the cows and calves, all blown, baffled, and still irritated with their senseless systematic revolt, circle uneasily about the yard. The staid old milker who had originated and fomented all the weary mischief lunged out wickedly whenever any calf but her own came within range of her horns. The dog, dead beat, but still ready to martyr himself for duty, lay down and fell to extracting the burrs from his hot feet. The horse, though his breath still came hurriedly, dozed, and, as his head dropped, roused the man with a pluck at the bridle. Then the tired stockman went across the trodden flat that lay between the stockyard and the house, lifting each heavy foot with a conscious effort, while the dog slunk dutifully behind, and the weary horse hung back drowsily on the bridle. The homestead buildings looked black and still against the stars. The man, having turned loose his horse, fought with the powers of sleep while he cast off his clothes; he lay down, stretched his long limbs once, then his hands fell slack, even before they had pulled the blankets to his chin.

Time was blotted out for him until he suddenly awoke with all his senses crystal-clear, to stare upon the patch of sky set in the open window-frame where the stars were dissolving in the dawn, and to wonder with suspended breath what was the unaccustomed sound that had brought him out of sleep. It was something clear and faint, befitting the early twilight, clear as a call in his ear, but light as a breath.

Then immediately it sounded again—it was a slow footstep on the garden path beneath his window. It stopped, and he heard the faintest whisper, as of falling folds of drapery. Some one was stooping among the plants; someone, and it was a woman, was humming cosily to herself. But who? This was not Aunt Martha's way, nor yet her voice; besides, Aunt Martha was not here. Surely, last night that black homestead had been untenanted—now who, or what——

He threw back his blankets, and swung out his feet to the earthen floor—temperament and training had combined by now to teach him the art of silence. He moved along the floor, and watched the pattern of the little treasured garden-plots. As he advanced, the walks and the well-known plants and bushes came stealthily into view, with the solemn dawn-look on them all, from beneath his window-frame. Then—most wondrous thing—one by one he saw besides a mazy curve of hair, loose-knotted, with a pink ear half hidden in its masses, and the line of temple, cheek, and chin of the quarter-face of a girl in white, who was stooping down to run slim white fingers amongst the leaves in the little bed of English violets. She plucked none, but parted the leaves here and there, and looked down upon the few shy and struggling alien blossoms, while she sang to herself in the woman's way—little unpremeditated minor cadences.

The face of the man at the window showed at first a still amaze, and then was wrung as if with pain.

She rose to her feet, and he withdrew stealthily, keeping his eyes upon her as he groped for garments to cover his nakedness. When his hands had found these, he stole to a corner in line with the window, and dressed in fearful and silent haste. When he crept to the window for another look, she was standing in the broadening light with her back to him, and with the fingers of the right hand loosely holding the left forefinger behind her, while with head tilted backward, so that the knot of her hair was pressed among the gauzy stuff about her neck, she seemed to watch the last few lingering stars as they melted out of the brightening firmament.

As the man came out of his room and went sidling down the length of the bachelors' quarters towards the kitchen at the other end, keeping as

GOING A-MILKING

far as possible out of sight of the holy ground of the garden where he had seen the Dawn Maiden, the whole sky-line was already ringed about with a girdle of primrose light that deepened towards the point of sunrise into golden-tawny, topped by a rosy flush.

It was midway in the hour of peace that falls with morning upon the Bush, and lasts from dawn until the sun has cleared the tree-tops; the uneasy things of the night-time had hidden themselves, and the daylight pests of earth and air were waiting for the warmth to thaw their numbness. Down in the wide resounding chasm of the creek, the laughing jackasses rolled out their laughter in full chorus, and a magpie high overhead fluted and gurgled his song of the sunrise, while from the stockyard came in phon and antiphon the full voices of the laden milkers outside the rails, and the heart-searching, hungry baby notes of the calves, made more penetrating by the calf-pen roof that acted as a sounding-board.

From the bench outside the kitchen door, where the milking buckets stood bottom upwards, ready for whosoever should do the Sunday milking, to the yards there were two ways—one by the smithy; the other, and much the longer, round by the garden wall and the house. The man examined the buckets with extravagant care for signs of the dregs of former milkings.

He was five feet ten, and a Saxon; nevertheless he whispered, with his head deep in one of the pails, "O God, who is it? A girl! A white girl! A lady! And I am an unclean beast. I'll go"—he ended, taking a bucket handle firmly in each hand—"round by the smithy." And with a firm step, and striving vainly after an appearance of unconsciousness, he started for the milking-yard, going by way of the garden.

He passed along the rear of the quarters, gripping his buckets desperately. The white figure was still in the garden; he looked straight ahead, and would have passed grimly without turning, but the Dawn Maiden first turned sharply as he appeared, and then ran for him with a little cry.

"Ned," she called, as she ran, holding out both hands, "Ned!" And then, as they faced one another across the wall, and he looked without moving, she thrust her two hands impulsively towards him. "Ned, speak to me!—it *is* you, isn't it?"

The two metal buckets fell with a clang, and he took her hands.

"Susie," he said quietly, and looked at her so long and so strangely that she flushed at last

GOING A-MILKING

suddenly over neck and face, and plucked lightly at her hands. He loosed them at once, and picked up the buckets.

"Listen what a row there is going on at the yards," he said. "I must go and milk at once"; and he stood back from the wall, showing her his full length, and looking somewhat sternly in the direction of the yards and the hoarse tumult. "I'm milkman to-day;" he brought his feet together as if gathering himself up for a resolute move to his work.

She read an invitation in the pause. "Going a-milking, Ned? Oh, may I come too, kind sir?—I'll be good," she added breathlessly.

Ned looked up and scanned her with a masterful, critical air, just as he used to do when she begged to be allowed to go with him on one of his boyish foraging expeditions.

"Oh, yes," he said; "but you'd better bring a wide hat if you have one. I'll let the dogs go and meet you at the house door."

When she came out, tying the ribbons of a broad-brimmed hat beneath her chin, he was waiting for her, and behind him there sat erect and exceedingly stern two great rough grey-blue dogs, who both rose as she appeared and came over to her. They both sniffed at her skirts and swung their tails respectfully, giving her, with drooping ears, a steady stare from beneath shaggy eyebrows out of rich brown eyes, deep with unfathomable depths of solemnity and devotion to duty, but tempered with a hint of humour, severely repressed until the fit and proper moment should arrive for giving way to it.

"That's Bim," Ned explained, as Susie patted the head of one, who moistened his lips delicately; "and that's Blucher," as she rubbed the right ear of the other, who looked up in her face, and gave mouth to a laboured hollow sound that was neither a yowl nor a yawn nor a bark, but was composed of all three.

"It's all right," Ned expounded seriously, as the girl started slightly; "that runs in Blucher's family, that noise. They're a nervous breed. He's letting you know he acknowledges you as a station hand." They had moved towards the stockyard as he spoke, and both the dogs were tacking across and across at their heels with a pre-occupied air.

Sounds of trumpetings and a babel of querulous undertones arrested Ned, and Susie followed him to a little outhouse on their right. He raised a shutter in the door, and a gaudy, martial-looking cock appeared upon the threshold, tilting his head to scan the group outside suspiciously with a bright, severe red eye, while the crowding congregation of fowls within hustled him forward as they streamed out in single file and scattered away to forage.

"I know it's late," Ned explained apologetically, as the cock cluttered witheringly at him; "but it's Sunday, you see, and you know what happens sometimes if we leave your front door open and the dingoes get in."

When they neared the stockyard, the early sunlight, fretted by the trees, had barred the whole face of the plain with golden arabesques, and their own shadows had come to stalk, lank and interminable, like new-created, formless things, beside them on the ground. At the further side, about the milking-yard, the answering choruses had grown to a persistent, clamorous din. As they rounded the massive corner-post of the stockyard they beheld several elderly, deep-bodied cows and two less experienced heifers in a row, all with their faces close to the rails, all bellowing together distractedly, while in the open entrance of the milking-yard a firm-set, short-horned matronly cow stood broadside-on, solidly barring the way with the superior manner of a policeman. Her eyes were half closed and her cheeks bulging as she chewed blandly at her cud; but as the milking party came in sight she swallowed her mouthful prematurely and faced about, with the instinctive obstinacy of her race, setting her tail where—according to the rule of right, reason and expediency, and the prompting of her own maternal wants and desires—her head should have been : that is, inside the yard. All the other animals followed her lead, and came to the right-about in a sudden silence, forming themselves up in what Susie took to be a charging line. She hung behind Ned for one terrified instant in the shelter of the great corner-post, but was at his shoulder again before he had noticed her lagging ; and she went on with him steadily, though her heart seemed to be in her throat.

He pulled up, keeping well back from the cows in the unprotected open, and began to harangue them sternly on the evils of insubordination. Susie was shaking in every limb, and unconsciously pressed lightly against him.

" Susie ! " He turned to her wonderingly. " What is it ? "

" I'm—I'm—fr——" She swallowed the word, but sent a scared look along the embattled line of horns. " Won't they t—trample you ? "

He shut his teeth hard upon the beginnings of a laugh. " You're at the antipodes," he said gently. " Everything's upside down here. Bush cattle, remember, run *from* you unless they're cornered and terrified—never *at* you."

GOING A-MILKING

Her shivering had ceased instantly. The blood flowed back to her cheeks. She would have pinched the hairy brown arm nearest to her, but Ned had turned away and was storming at the cows, who had now broken up their fighting formation, and were making for the gate, where the officious matron, still firmly planted, kept them at bay with her horns.

"That's Maamie," said Ned, as the old cow retired before the press of numbers, still doggedly fencing, "boss of the milking-yard just at present, and only happy when she's being a nuisance."

The last to come to the open gate was one of the younger heifers, who was in a condition of extreme nervousness when she arrived there. She would have passed in peacefully, but that Maamie, spying her nervousness, and realising that here was the last opportunity likely to offer on this occasion for lodging her protest against order and good government, plunged forward and planted a horn firmly against the timid heifer's brisket. The frightened creature swung away, and the fear in her mounted up to terror when she saw that the man, the dogs, and, worse than all, the fearful white skirt, had drawn up and were close upon her. The crimson fire flamed out in her eyes; she gave one mad bellow, and charged for the open wilds. The hot blast of the heifer's breath as she charged by set the girl's skirts swinging.

Susie looked open-eyed at the danger till it was past, and then, still feeling the protecting arm about her that had swung her aside, she buried her face unashamed in Ned's neck, and clung to his shoulder and sobbed noiselessly. "Blucher! Bim! Fetch her back," she heard above her, and felt the sinewy throat vibrate against her ear to the words as the scurry of the dogs' flying feet died away.

She clung a little tighter, but did not lift her head as the arm about her half carried her into the yard. Presently she turned her head quietly, without raising it, and caught for an instant a foreshortened glimpse of the face above her, the view that intensifies the expression of a face by concentrating the features, as we read those attenuated puzzle-writings by tilting the card and setting the letters end-on. He must have thought her eyes still hidden. The face had a lost, fell look upon it. Somehow he had armed himself with a heavy stick, and the right hand holding it was raised to strike; the left still held her to him. To strike, with a face like that, was to do murder, and Susie raised a hand and cried out as the stick fell with a hideous hollow blow on—on the nose of Maamie, who had sought to follow the absconding heifer and leave the yard.

GOING A-MILKING

Susie raised her bewildered head, and was pushed gently into the shelter of the corner post. The heifer was coming at a headlong gallop for the yard, with Bim and Blucher biting at her heels like avenging fiends.

As the three shot within the angle of the yards, the dogs desisted at Ned's command, and came on quietly like two uncoupled railway cars behind a locomotive, while the heifer thundered on into the sanctuary of the yard, to be met by a prod from the irreconcilable Maamie and by smothered mutterings of sympathy from the other cows. Bim and Blucher sat down side by side, rolling their heads and panting luxuriously, with an air of congratulating one another on the successful spin.

Ned closed the gate, and then, with a hand upon it, he stood a while looking down at his clumsy boot as it swung backwards and forwards, smoothing the rumpled sand.

Susie had her anxious attention on the humiliated heifer, and on this new perplexity of Ned's behaviour, in turn. The chorus of cows and calves had broken out afresh, now that no further postponement of milking seemed possible.

"Susie," he said, looking up at her so quickly that she jumped; "it's such a beastly rough welcome. No, no, you're all right," he added, fol-

DINKINBAR

lowing her eyes, "now the brute's safe in the yard. But—but—*is* it you ? is it you really ? "

"Goodness, Ned!" she returned, aghast almost, after what had already passed at the return of his first amaze at seeing her; "who else ? Haven't we let out the fowls, and didn't you introduce me to the dogs, and save my life from that wild beast ? What in the—— Oh !"—she looked at him with parted lips—"it's not possible you didn't *know* I was coming."

"I didn't, then."

"Ned, you got no letters at Melbourne ?"

"I—I didn't go to Melbourne." He looked down, as it seemed to her, guiltily.

"And when you saw me in the garden ?"

"I had no——" He looked out gravely through the gate, across the plain. "I thought you were——"

"What, Ned? A—a what ? Tell me ?"

"I thought you were a spirit. I did. I called you the—the—you'll laugh."

"Ah, Ned!"

"The Dawn Maiden, then."

He was still looking out across the plain.

She answered with a little cooing, like slurred notes on a muted string.

"But I did," he went on doggedly, like a schoolboy reluctantly confessing his sins.

"And you didn't know me?" She made a little wondering shake of the head.

He was smoothing the sand with his boot again, and watching it earnestly. He shook his head slowly. In the rusty, rumpled hat-crown that was presented to her, there was a jagged hole. He looked almost loutish when he stooped that way, she thought, what with the burst hat and baggy shirt and trousers, showing gathered stains of many perfunctory cold-water washings in them, and the big boots. And yet, an instant ago, her finest sympathies had thrilled in answer to him when he had called her.

She stamped her foot at him. "Ned!" she called from the borderland of tears, "it's all so queer. You—you knew me when I called you—you took my hands?" The ragged hat-crown nodded slowly. "And all of a sudden it was like old times again."

He did not look up, but he seemed to join with her in the dim chase after words to voice their mutual bewilderment. "It was," he answered carefully, "after the first look—after I dropped the buckets. Only—only there was a wall between us," he added in a harder voice. "But to find *you* in the garden at Dinkinbar—well, it was too wonderful to begin to try and talk about it. Wasn't it?"

This was better, she felt. They had both, with tactful, consenting silence, during that first unfathomable pause, run back the trail of the vanished years to that point far back in their lives where their paths had been one; there, as boy and girl, they had joined hands.

They would go back again now. "It was, oh, it was," she agreed joyfully, yielding up the lead to him.

"It just seemed as if we had turned boy and girl again," he said with comrade-like garrulity, and looked out between the gate-bars; "it seemed the only thing to do."

It was the very marrow of her thought. "It took away all the awkwardness," she concurred with heartiness. "The dogs seemed to know me for—for your old chum, Ned."

He glanced at her with an answering sparkle, but turned his eye to the plain again. "Like Mop. Remember Mop, Sue?"

"Remember! The way I wept when he got himself tarred somehow, and you threatened to put a match to him unless I lent you my—was it my paint-box?"

"No—the little beast that I was—some sewing arrangement you had," he corrected. "I had my eye on the silk in it, and I remember I stole it nearly all."

GOING A-MILKING

"Nonsense!" she returned almost warmly; "besides, it did me good, and look at the lots of things you gave me. I believe Mop saved my life, though, the way he tore off for the kitchen, barking frantically, and pulled at the maid's clothes the time I fell into the—the—oh! I forget."

"I remember. By the cow-house. Call it the liquid fertiliser."

As he uttered his euphemism, he looked up to find her eyes fixed on him in a little spasm of childish horror at the awkwardness of that last reminiscence of their youth.

They broke simultaneously into a laugh, that sobered, however, into a long, deep gaze of mutual wonderment. It seemed as though they stood each one a child, each surveying the other with reverential awe as one who had grown to full, remote, mysterious man- and womanhood in a single night.

"Poor old ragged Mop!" she continued presently, but dreamily rather, for their eyes still clung together, dealing in mysteries. "Yes, he saved me from a liq—a watery grave that time. And you, Ned, you saved my life this morning. Now there—we're grown up, but look—just think how like it all is to old times; look at the way I flung myself into your arms when that animal frightened me just now. Fancy me doing that with a stranger! It's just like old times still, isn't it, Ned?"

For many seconds he continued to gaze at her, answering nothing, and her cheeks grew hot. "No," he said at last, "it isn't!"

She remembered, as he spoke, that foreshortened view of his face and the lost look upon it. Something of the look had returned, but with more in it of forlornness than of rage. That guide-rope of the past was slipping from her; she clutched at it desperately.

"But it is, it is," she cried pleadingly. "See here, Ned, it was all my fault—some strange feeling. But look how big you're grown, and with a beard, and so brown. I think you almost frightened me. But look how soon I found you, the same old—old—dear old—brave old—Ned I've come all the way to s—see." The "s" came to her tongue for "save," but she made a lightning change. "Look how I clung to you when there was danger, just as I used to. What difference can there be?"

"Stop, Sue, stop!" he said hoarsely, and a bucket he had stooped to lift clattered in his hand. "That was it, just that, when you clung to me, that showed me. It seemed as if it might be like old times till then. But, you remember there was a wall between us. Oh, there's a

GOING A-MILKING

world. I saw it then. I'm an uncl—" (he remembered his own voice in the hollow of the bucket, and he, too, changed the word), "an uncouth beast. And you're a—a—I think I'm frightened of you." His utterance tripped between weak laughter and a sob.

"I'm Sue, your old Sukie, there!" she said defiantly. "We've climbed trees, Ned, you and I; we can still manage stone walls. Fie, oh you goose! And travelling's easy now—the width of the world shan't keep old friends apart. Do you see me, sir?"

She drew up straight and slim, and held her skirts to her and tossed her head back. The broad hat threw a wavy line of shade from temple to chin; shadow and sun showed up the face in a subtle and eminently kissable variety of winsomeness.

She made as if to run into his arms, and for an instant his face brightened; but he stepped back immediately, swinging the bucket between them, and turned to the gate again with a scowl in his forehead that might lie upon the faces of the lost and damned, or might signify merely coltish diffidence and a boyish horror of caresses. In the next instant he was shouting welcomes to the incarnation of matter-of-fact that had strolled into his sight in the form of Mr. Joseph Heyrick.

CHAPTER VI

The Tyranny of Trifles

"HUL-L-O-O there!" Ned roared joyfully; "if it isn't Uncle Joe!"

"Hullo, lad, hullo!" Uncle Joseph answered reposefully and without hurrying. "Morning, Susie. Found him, have you? Middling fit, Ned, eh?"

"Middling. And you—you're more than middling fat, Uncle Joe."

"None of your impudence."

By this time Uncle Joseph had been admitted into the yard. The two men surveyed one another carefully from top to toe. Uncle Joseph's hands did not stir from his coat pockets, and Ned likewise made no advance towards a handshaking. Susie looked on at the laconic greeting with an air, outwardly, of lively interest. Uncle Joseph turned to her with sternly repressed pride. "Like a chunk of ironbark, isn't he, Susie?" Then he nodded towards the main stockyard. "What's the little mob of cows and calves in there for?"

THE TYRANNY OF TRIFLES

"Ho-ho!" laughed Ned; "mean to say you've forgotten old Strawberry Jam that nearly killed me when we broke her in? You'll forget the name of the station next."

"Forget your grandmother's needle!" Uncle Joseph returned hotly. "I'd as soon forget my prayers; 's if I didn't know every old milker on the run. Must have been behind the other ones, she must."

"Of course; that's like Strawberry Jam's modesty, isn't it? I brought the others to break in for milkers. Nice job they gave me to drive, too.—I say, Uncle Joe," he added comfortingly, "it's all right; I won't let on to these chummies of yours that you don't know your own——" But here, with a well-judged kick, Uncle Joseph sent the empty bucket spinning from Ned's hand.

"He's clean out of hand, the brat," the old squatter remarked beamingly to Susie. "And I'll let the chummies know," he stormed at Ned, "that milking on this run's got to be over by sunrise, or thereabout. Look at you!—not a cow milked, and it's close on breakfast-time."

Ned had rushed away, and was now by the milking-bail vigorously dusting out the buckets. Susie drifted doubtfully towards the gate. Mr. Heyrick looked from one to the other, and rubbed his beard. "Eh, to be sure," he said confusedly.

She ran back to him. "To be sure it was I; I kept him from his work. Think of the time it is since we've seen one another."

She fled from the yard, and for a little from outside it she watched the two men at their occupation.

Ned was soon on the milking-stool with his head buried in the capacious flank of Maamie, whose pent-up milk was purring softly and freely into the bucket between his knees. Maamie, seeing no prospect of creating further disturbances after the closing of the gate, had promptly horned a more timid applicant for the comforts of first milking out of the bail, and had established herself in position there, where she had blandly continued her interrupted cud-chewing. Ned's voice came hollowly out from the cow's flank as he responded to Uncle Joseph's curt, comprehensive comments and inquiries concerning stock, grass, water, the neighbours, the iniquities of recent and prospective land legislation, or his projects for utilising the new-chum labour to the best advantage of Dinkinbar. Maamie was milked and let go. Ned rose to bail up the next cow, tied her hind leg back to the fence, and instructed Uncle Joseph, who stood guard over the gate of the calf-pen, which calf to let out of all those watching hungrily for their turn. During these manœuvres both men sent Susie a friendly look, and answered her questions on the mysteries of Bush milking. But after the calf had been allowed at once to start the milk flowing in its natural way and to take the first edge off its hunger, and when Uncle Joseph had slipped the hide rope about its neck and had pulled it away, allowing Ned to continue his milking, then they both fell to again, zestfully, upon affairs of station business, and seemed to forget the girl. The third chosen candidate for milking was the heifer that had frightened Susie. The animal cast a look of fearful suspicion when she saw the white skirt outside, and swerved from the bail. Susie, with the memory of her terror new in her, shuddered back from the rails. Ned, with his back to Uncle Joseph, in one quick message signalled comfortingly to her, and at the same time, with an infinitesimal frown and a shake of the head, conveyed that the story of her fright had best remain their secret. Then the two men were re-absorbed by their men's affairs, and the girl slipped away unnoticed.

The loneness that comes to those who are projected suddenly as idlers amongst preoccupied and busy friends fell heavily upon Susie as she left the yard. The sun had climbed so far that, as she went slowly to the house, the shadow at her side had shrunk to credible proportions; a column of blue smoke bustled straight in air from the throat of the kitchen chimney, and the early flies were plaguing her ears and face.

The smoke, the normal shadow, and the awakened flies stood with her for the continuance of the dull invasion of daily uninspiring things, headed by the arrival of good, thick-headed Uncle Joseph at the yard, that had blundered in upon her free, fresh intercourse with Ned.

The common things had arrived with deadly inopportuneness on the instant when she was in the very act of wringing the acknowledgment from him that the old full-hearted comradeship of their hobbledyhoydom was left untouched by long severance and unfettered by the flight of years. That once established, she would have regained in the act her old position at his side as sister and playfellow.

Apart from the dreadful glint in his eyes as of one fallen from his caste; his rumpled clothing, and the mute and clumsy bearing of him when he felt called upon to apply some little touch of the arts and graces of civility towards her, were more than a tenfold justification for her bringing all her feminine arts to bear upon him for his reclamation.

THE TYRANNY OF TRIFLES

As she had drawn herself up in challenge of his admiration, her mission—and the more than urgent need of it now that its object was before her—and all that had led her to embark upon it had shone before her clear in mind and memory, back to the morning when Jim had discoursed easily across the breakfast table on Bush living and its attendant evils.

All that was but a moment ago, and yet now, as she flicked restlessly with her handkerchief at the besieging flies, an age of time and an ocean of hindrances seemed to lie between her and the instant when Uncle Joseph had rounded the corner of the milking-yard, had hindered her from bringing Ned to the acceptance of her point of view by the arguments of kissing and hugging, since the mere look of her had not been all-compelling, and since the two men had joined together, first in rude welcome of one another, then in horseplay, then in absorbed discussion of men's affairs so alien to her. She beat helplessly about amongst the mighty, mean obstructions that had suddenly overwhelmed her.

The look of the house, agape at every opening along its low, ramshackle length, smote upon her mood with a chill unfriendliness. It faced to the eastward, so that the front might be sheltered from the glare of afternoon, and now the early sunlight lay bleakly along the whole length of the billowy clay floor of the verandah.

Along the timbers of the bald front was written —Uncle Joseph had told her the story last night—the rise and progress of the house of Heyrick at Dinkinbar. To the right of the door the wall was of weather-board, layered and trim, with the curved tracks upon it where the circular saw had bitten and screamed its way through the timber; the two windows there were glazed, and the front was dandified with a coat of white paint. But to the left of the central doorway there still stood, weather-worn and grey, erect, shoulder to shoulder like veterans on parade, the old original slabs, their feet sunk in mother earth, rough-hewn from the log, with the marks of axe and adze still clear upon them. They still held above them the first rafters and the first roof-tree that had sheltered the Dinkinbar pioneers, Uncle Joseph and his wife. Half a dozen narrow loop-holes the height of a man's shoulder—though they had been boarded up on the inside this many a year—still recalled the possible need of defence by the rifle-barrel. Although the whole long roof was now one drear level of white-painted corrugated iron, Uncle Joseph had told how, when the last covering of bark had been stripped to make way for the modern innovation of weather-proof metal, he thought he heard the naked, venerable rafters groan, how Aunt Martha had cried, and how he himself had turned away blood-guiltily.

Last night, as she had sat at his knee looking out upon the starlit plain, drinking in the story, and listening for a horse's footfall, it had seemed to her that Romance had for once come down from her shining peaks to meet the Real. And now, alack! what with the hard sunlight, the strange elusive happenings of the morning and the rush of trivial things, the humble monument of the fortunes of Dinkinbar seemed half sordid, half cheap. Blucher and Bim had followed her demurely to the house, since, apparently, proceedings at the milking-yard had become hopelessly tame. One of them was thoughtfully scratching his chest; the other, engaged in a flea-hunt, was emitting wallowy, snoring sounds behind her. She turned fiercely upon them in a sudden tempest of irritation. Both looked up, hung their ears, and swept their tails in abject apology. It is in our moments of keenest sensibility that the eyes and the ways of brutes are most tragically appealing. Under the two dogs' eyes Susie grew sore ashamed, and ran inside, calling for Aunt Martha.

A voice answered her from the depths of the store, which was at the rear and in a far corner of the old section of the house. Aunt Martha was there, short-skirted, plain-clad, the embodiment of implacable housewifery. She was white to the elbows, and stood up as Susie came in, from making a rigorous search in an open flour-bag.

The sense of strangeness fell upon the girl more smartingly than before, the feeling of all tenderness being crushed by the insistent multitude of raw, rude, material things; for at first Aunt Martha, fresh from the inspection of the flour-bag, turned upon her the eyes of a martinet on duty.

"Weevils!" she said sternly, then sought for an unfloured spot on her right forearm, on which to rub the bridge of her nose. That done, however, she looked up with a softened face. " Have you slept, child ? Dick tells me Ned came home in the night; have you seen him ? Ah, you're feeling strange, my lammie—there, I knew it when you called. No wonder—it makes us rough and heedless. Kiss me, dearie, but mind the flour—— Oh, but it does."

Aunt Martha resumed her stern examination of the flour-bag, and the girl watched her as she passed in her review to the tea, soap, and raisins, and the shelves crowded with tins and bottles. Everything was parasite-infested and in mannish disarray; and the housewife's muttered soliloquy boded ill for the venerable cook on the occasion of her next interview with him.

Mrs. Heyrick had started back in angry horror from an open sugar-sack alive with soldier ants, when the voices of Ned and Uncle Joseph reached her from the outside. Uncle Joseph was rating the younger man in his breezy manner.

"It's my boy, my boy; listen!" said Aunt Martha with her motherly thrill.

"No spell in town—missed the Races, not to mention the arrival of your friends and relations," Uncle Joseph was storming heartily. "Left all your letters lying. What in thunder——? Well, it licks me. Man!"—there fell the sound of an open-handed smack—"when I was your age"—then a whisper followed, and a horse-laugh—"and the girl coming"—another smack—"and the chummies; and you never knew. What d'you mean, lad, anyhow?"

"I couldn't"—Ned's voice came hesitatingly—"face the stink and the glare of a big town somehow——"

"What!"

"No, I mean—I thought I—I might as well have a look at those two or three lots of bulls we talked of, you know."

"Ah! but Lord, man——"

"And the boy fairly cried when he thought he

wouldn't see the Races, and I let him go. And look here, Uncle Joe," with sudden defiance, "I hankered after the station anyway, and the—and your infernal bullocks topped the market; and there's not a mickey [1] or a broken fence or gate on the run. So there you are; and you can like it or do the other thing."

"The run's topping, but it licks me, all the same," said Uncle Joseph doggedly.

Aunt Martha had listened, looking with a curious intensity at Susie all the time, and with her floury hands hanging loosely before her. "Bless the boy!" she said at last, and ran out when the voices sounded loudly in the back passage.

Susie hung back for a moment; she looked round the untidy store smiling distractedly, and when Uncle Joseph called jovially for her she pressed her open hands to her temples before she went to him.

[1] "Mickey," a bull calf which, through careless or inefficient stockmanship, has been missed, and has grown big while still unbranded.

CHAPTER VII

Sunday on Dinkinbar

THE Sunday afternoon was well advanced before the girl from England found relief from the tyranny of trifles—as it seemed to her—that had held dominion over her and the Dinkinbar homestead from the moment when Uncle Joseph appeared at the milking-yard until he and Aunt Martha went for their afternoon nap.

Then she hurried to her room, got out writing materials, and firmly set down on a sheet of notepaper the cattle-station's name, the date, and underneath, " My darling Jim." She pressed the end of the penholder to her under-lip, and frowned determinedly through the open window-frame across the staring sand, where the bleached stockyard rails shimmered mirage-like in the sunshine. It was to her the first performance of the daily task to which she had vowed her sternest resolution, that of keeping fresh and unflawed in this wild place the home associations, for her own and others' good. All through the morning and the forenoon, whenever she had been able to snatch a moment's reflection, she had longed for solitude and the liberty to detach herself from the things about her, that she might by serious, consciously-directed effort mark the first stage towards the accomplishment of that errand of mercy she had travelled half the world to execute. She planted an elbow firmly on each side of her note-paper, closed her teeth lightly on the penholder, and fell hungrily upon her recollections of the day's doings and her own part in them, sternly resolved to extract from her review some concise, clear-drawn conclusion which should help her to watchfulness of her attitude and actions in the future development of her scheme for the reclamation of Dinkinbar to gentler ways of living.

From that first meeting by the garden wall she seemed removed by an infinity of time; and yet it alone stood clear and unconfused before her. Passing onward from that moment, purpose and memory parted company, and a mass of bewildering and irrelevant detail swarmed in upon her recollection, making a deliberate survey impossible. There were the solemn cattle-dogs, the rush of the frightened heifer, and the new Ned, with his inscrutable changing humour, now fierce, hard, and bitter, as when she had seen him while clinging to his neck, now full of a yearning gentleness and wonder, as when she had intercepted one of

SUNDAY ON DINKINBAR

his timid side-looks at her, and again of baffling simplicity as he harangued the milkers or apologised to the domineering rooster. And then, that marvellous interview by the gate, that seemed to her now to have been carried on in dumb show, or in some lost language, for not a word of it could she recall; and what in the name of wonder had bidden her, as if from instinctive jealousy of some unknown rival, to flash upon him the display of her charms? She thought of it without the hint of a blush; but if Uncle Joseph had not arrived, and if her impulse to give Ned that sisterly hug had not been checked, would she have remembered as calmly as now? But she was hurried on to the bluff greeting of the men to one another after such long absence, and thenceforward the happenings of the morning galloped by in ever-increasing confusion.

She roused herself at last from a somewhat shamefaced recollection of the shock inflicted upon her daintiness by the plainness and plenteousness of the Dinkinbar breakfast, the weight and thickness of the white tea-cups, and the enormous tin teapot—so like a watering-can—to find herself gazing with wide-open eyes towards the stockyard, while, with her head slowly turning from side to side, she was industriously engaged in trying to make the butt of her penholder rap out, as it ran across her teeth, the lilt and measure of the air of "Father O'Flynn."

She frowned severely out upon the sunlit expanse, and made to put the right punctuation to the superscription of her letter. The ink was dry on the pen, and a large purple-red ant was standing on the rim of her inkpot, looking in and twiddling its feelers as if admiring its reflection. She rose up angrily and stepped back, with her eyes fastened on the intruder, and, holding the penholder at arm's length, she waited till the ant cautiously lowered itself for closer observation of the contents of the inkbottle, and tipped it in. But when she looked in guiltily and saw the insect looking up with a tiny, pitifully-stupid face, and pawing helplessly with inky legs at the glass, she ran horror-stricken from the room.

Ned, with a gun on his shoulders and with Bim at his heels, was crossing from the bachelors' quarters.

"Ned, Ned!" she called wildly; "there's a beast in my room."

He ran up and stood in the doorway with his gun at the ready. "What is it—where?" he asked.

"An ant—in the inkpot!" she fluttered almost inaudibly behind him.

"In the——" She did not see whether he turned to behold her humiliation, for she was gazing at the floor; but in her soul she thanked

SUNDAY ON DINKINBAR

him for his silence as he set down the gun, and she looked up in time to see that he took off the crumpled hat and looked neither to the right nor to the left as he entered the room and went over to the table. He fished out the ant on the penholder, shook it off as he left the room, and set his foot upon it.

She put her hands to her ears to hide the small sounds of crunching, then looked at the little mutilated body in dismay, shuddered at the sight of the clumsy, shapeless boot that had mangled it, and recoiled almost imperceptibly.

Ned replaced the shabby hat, pushing the wavy brim over his eyes, took up his antiquated muzzle-loading gun, and started for the open doorway, where Bim was sitting with tilted head in a ferment of curiosity, making small, tense, whistling sounds in his nose.

Ned's back was no sooner turned than the girl longed to say something to recall him; but he trudged stolidly out into the sun, and snapped his fingers once as he passed the dog, whether to call him to heel or in contempt of her childishness the girl could not tell. She stood tongue-tied as he retreated. Bim marked time uneasily with his paws, as if the earth burned, and saluted humbly with his ears up into Susie's face and towards his master's slowly retreating figure in turn.

Suddenly the dog took a watching air, and a faint sound of voices and the trampling of horses reached the girl's ears.

"Ned," she called imperiously, "come here! There's somebody coming," she added faintly, as he turned half round and lowered his gun-butt on the sand. Bim touched her finger-tips demurely with his tongue, then raced round to the front of the house, barking furiously.

"I expect it's these new-chums of yours," Ned remarked, dourly the girl thought, as she ran through the house.

A loose procession of five mounted men was coming across the plain, the leading four exhibiting every variety of inelegance in their horsemanship; for, as the girl came out on the front verandah, Jim Baxter, the stockman, who brought up the rear, let loose his stockwhip, and sounded it in a succession of reports as if a heavy revolver had been fired, causing the four new-chums' horses to set off at a free hand-gallop for the house.

Aplin in the lead, who had taken off his enormous new felt hat to wave it to the girl, dropped it and laid hold of his horse's mane with both hands; Hulbert, with his elbows squared out as he held the reins close beneath his armpits, shot up woodenly out of the saddle at every stride; Finlay let go his reins and clung wildly with both

SUNDAY ON DINKINBAR

hands to the pommel; Creswell alone, with little dignity but much determination, got a short grip of his reins, with the slack of the leather bunched between his hands, and set his knees firm. When he arrived at the verandah he had his teeth shut, but his horse alone of the four was in hand. The stockman, having started his cavalcade, reined up his horse, leaned his forehead on its neck, and shouted with laughter.

The fresh faces of the four new-chums, their open delight at seeing her again, and their boyish pride in the wild horsemanship as they all climbed stiffly down, appealed gratefully to the girl as something wholesome and simple after the tragic confusion and lonesomeness which the day's immersion in the new conditions had brought upon her. She forgot her soreness and humiliation at the pitiful breakdown of her first daily judicial summing-up of the new life, and how she was to discharge her mission to mitigate its harshness, in offering her delighted sympathy as the new-chums poured out to her the tale of their journey up to Dinkinbar, and what a rattling time they had had, and meant to have, in this bigger world. With the exception of Creswell, who still maintained something of his customary solidity and shrewdness of manner, they were all superlatively enthusiastic; and in their dazzling moleskins and voluminous, open-necked shirts, fresh out of the Bingo stores, all but Creswell lounged, and posed, and appeared to regard themselves as daring and finished frontiersmen.

Aplin crossed his legs, leaned against his horse's shoulder, threw an arm across its neck, and toyed with the mane.

"What a magnificent fellow Snelling is!" he said. "That's what I call an Englishman with all the nonsense taken out of him. He says England's played out, except as a kind of museum, and——" but the horse edged away, and Aplin had some difficulty in recovering his balance.

The owner of Dinkinbar was jolted from the blissful depths of his Sunday nap by the cyclonic arrival of the new-chums, their noisy, unprofessional manner of dismounting, and their high-pitched volubility under the verandah.

He tossed aside the mosquito curtains, silently thrust a rumpled and exasperated head through the open window-frame, and became an unnoticed spectator of the scene outside.

The four young Englishmen were all bidding vociferously for the girl's notice. Jim Baxter, the stockman, in the middle distance was leading his horse to the saddle-room, having exchanged a seemly, laconic greeting with Ned, who, with his dog and gun, had turned his back upon the new

SUNDAY ON DINKINBAR

arrivals, and was disappearing amongst the lank, sad-coloured undergrowth that fringed the creek-side.

As Mr. Heyrick removed his irritated scrutiny from the two seasoned bushmen in the background to the noisy group at his elbow, Aplin's eulogium of the fascinating Snelling fell upon his ears.

"That's his way of putting it. Snelling didn't happen to remark, did he," the squatter said to the group outside, his voice husky with sleep, "that if a man happens to be born a forty,[1] he finds decent company in England a bit too hot to hold him?"

The four new-chums stared round at the window, dumbfounded at this reception. Hitherto the squatter's geniality, and his tolerance of the ways of young men, had promised well for their term of colonial experience under him; this was their first sight of him in the *rôle* of the captain expounding, in the manner of a skipper, the sacredness of his own quarter-deck.

All the young men fell into a silence, and looked part sheepish, part resentful, except Creswell, who, with unstirred equanimity, murmured under his breath to Susie, "How odd! I'd no idea Snelling

[1] "Forty": a professional sharper. The origin of the term is doubtful, though it has been sought to trace some connection with "Ali Baba and the Forty Thieves."

was born so far ahead of his era. I should have said Forty by effluxion of time."

Uncle Joseph, having cleared his throat noisily, went on, " You young fellows had better get your saddles off, and——" He disappeared suddenly, as if pulled backwards, and from the room there issued subdued sounds of hasty discussion.

An awkward silence still reigned along the verandah, when Aunt Martha came briskly out and made the new-chums kindly welcome, soothing the ruffled ones with a show of real solicitude for their comfort in the new place.

" And where's Ned ? Have they seen him ? " she asked, turning to the girl, whose eyes went wandering confusedly round the empty landscape.

" Ay, where's Ned ?" Uncle Joseph repeated, as he came out, buttoning a creased and baggy coat.

As if in answer, the report of a gun, followed by crashing echoes and the frantic barking of a dog, resounded from the rocky hollows far up the creek-bed.

" H'm, duck-hunting he is, as usual of a Sunday," Mr. Heyrick said, and added absently, looking at Susie, " getting a lonely devil, is Ned ; time he had company round. Mind, you chaps," he said, addressing the new-chums generally, " I'll see to it that you work here ; but there's three things chiefly you've got to beware of on

SUNDAY ON DINKINBAR

your own account. One's dirt, and that's bad; and another's drink, and that's worse; and the third's loneliness—if you give in to *that*, and begin to turn hatter"—his wife plucked him by the sleeve—"like a horse or a bull gone sulky-mad, which is absurd, of course," he concluded hastily; and then, as if to show that all his remarks, including that from the window, had been mere conversational pleasantry and *apropos* of nothing in particular, he continued, retiring with manifest relief on practical matters, "Lead your horses round, boys, and I'll show you your camp and where you stow the saddles."

The women stayed behind. "What's a hatter, Aunt Martha?" Susie asked.

"A hatter, child?" The elder woman followed the younger one's look, which was roaming back and forth along the ragged line of the river-timber. Then their eyes met, and the girl repeated the question.

"A hatter?" Aunt Martha said, scanning the girl's face in a puzzled way. "Oh, when a horse or a beast gets queer and lonely, you know, and pokes away by himself, and won't feed with his mates, we say he's turned hatter, that's all;" and she made as if to draw the girl inside with her.

But Susie hung back. "Do *men* ever turn hatter? Do they?" she asked.

" Ay, they do, God help them!" the elder woman said in a hurried half-whisper, and as if an ugly secret had been forced from her. Then she hastened away, for Uncle Joseph was calling her.

The girl, left alone upon the long, clay-floored verandah, let her eyes travel bemusedly abroad. The fervour of the day's heat was spent by now, and the distance was no longer tortured and shuddering in the sun-haze. The mile-wide plain, and the low, timbered ridges that closed it round, shone dusky-orange, and the mighty framework of the stockyards to the right glinted like bar-gold in the steady glare; the shadow of the house was broadening to eastward, and out of the spiry, feathery she-oaks that bordered the creek-bed came the first pipings of the birds that were flocking in to drink.

The sound of another gunshot from far up the watercourse scattered silence amongst the birds, and a flock overhead, that had been skimming towards the water, wheeled in its course, and hurried from the direction of the sound.

Susie put an arm about one of the hacked and weather-bleached old verandah posts, and listened long as she watched the evening shades creeping out and drowning the sun-gold on the plain, stripping the stockyard of its gilded coat of flame-colour, and quenching from the earth upward the

SUNDAY ON DINKINBAR

tawny lustre of the she-oaks, till the topmost slender cone burned for a moment, a solitary beacon above the shadows, a last flicker in the closing eye of day.

While the spacious twilight deepened out of doors, the half-hour before supper was passed in the lamplit house in anything but conversational ease. Uncle Joseph was rendered socially impracticable by hunger, the unseemly absence of his head stockman, Ned, and the youthful buoyancy of certainly three of the new-chums.

Aunt Martha was ruffled and distraught after a series of warm encounters, in which she had come off second best, with the cynical old cook over the disorganized condition into which the household had drifted under his masculine ineptitude; she hinted her concern, besides, as to whether her manner of spending the day had not laid her open to a charge of Sabbath-breaking.

The rest, not far enough on in life to have reached and tried the refuge of silence, and with no choice open to them but speed when conversational substance was wanting and nerves might be ajar, were holding high talk round the lamp.

Susie, with a mind uncoupled from the present, and running uneasily and ineffectually back and forth among the strange occurrences of the day, from the morning's milking to the distant, solitary gunfire on the creek, had given over tongue and features to the entertainment of the young men, in order that the awkward pre-supper interval might be comfortably tided over. Being left to themselves, these attractive members were making the most of their opportunities, and showing a hundred tricks of lip and eye and the management of dimples, such as—notably if the lack of deep design that underlies the pretty wantonness be of the Irish persuasion—are eternally liable to misconstruction.

She was at the end of the long pine-board table, with the uncle and aunt behind her, and the new-chums sat in pairs at either side of her. Except Hulbert, who was next to her on the right, sitting with his hands beneath the table, and looking somewhat diffident and alarmed, they were all disposed to sprawl towards her on the table and to be somewhat noisy. Under the stress of her sub-conscious striving after conversational zest, the girl's tongue rattled brightly, and the colour glowed in her cheeks, and, with an uneasy feeling that the conversational ball she had started was somehow getting beyond her management, she nevertheless retorted upon a lumbering and somewhat heated vindication by Aplin of man's innate modesty with a ringing peal of laughter.

SUNDAY ON DINKINBAR

"I expect," Uncle Joseph cut in drily, "supper will be here in a minute, and perhaps you young people had better make room for Dick."

In the silence that followed, Susie looked with a deepened colour round the young men; she appeared on a sudden correct and severe; in truth, she was confused, and wondering as well whether a small sound that had come to her ears from without during the pause had been heard by any of the others. It was the whining of a dog. None of the rest seemed to have noticed it, and, making a feint of preparing for supper, she hurried out to the back door.

Ned, with a limp-hanging brace of ducks in his hand, stood still in the middle of the open, and Bim, sitting erect and stiff, was at his master's heels. Susie ran towards him, but he remained stock still, and the same vague impulse that had driven her to him in the milking-yard died out again before his unresponsiveness, so that she pulled up within two paces of him. The dog rose up, sniffed humbly at her skirts, and sat down between the pair, turning his head from one to the other.

"Where have you been?" she said faintly and breathlessly. "Why did you run away like that, Ned?"

He looked down and swung the dead birds slowly in his hand. "You seem pretty comfortable amongst them," he said. "I've lost the run of my company manners." She stamped and faced half round from him, and suddenly he looked up and addressed her frankly and peremptorily. "There, I'm a beast, Sue; but if you come tumbling into the garden that way out of nowhere, why, of course you bowl me out." He came forward a step. "I couldn't face the chummies just at once. It's all right now. But listen. You're just to have a jolly time out here. If I'd had notice that you were coming, I wouldn't have let you in for that stupid business this morning. Don't worry after old times and all that; they're dead and buried, and——"

"They're not," she said, facing him defiantly, with the nameless impulse of the morning again in full possession of her.

"But they are," he said quietly, "and this is good-bye to 'em. Just take things as you find them."

"I will not," she said, all the more vehemently because she did not know what it was against which she had entered into war. "I won't be cast off by old chums this way without a better reason."

He lost confidence somewhat, and looked about as if hoping for interruption. "Old chums? nonsense! I don't know," he said almost guiltily, "what you—what we're—making all this trouble about."

"Neither do I," triumphantly. "You see? There must be something you're hiding from me. Or else, in the milking-yard, just before Uncle Joseph came, how was it——?" She was brought up by her headlong rush upon the awkward recollection.

"There was nothing," he said, relapsing into doggedness, "except my clumsiness—nothing in the world."

She laughed a little in a puzzled way, wondering that his impenetrable moods merely inflamed her eagerness at hunting unknown objects in the dark. She set her hands upon her waist. "Then I'm going to find it," she said conclusively.

"For pity's sake don't look," he said appealingly.

"What matter? Aren't women born to look for nothing, and don't they generally find it?"

"I tell you," he said, still more uneasily, "I'm grown a plain, rough stock-rider, as plain as Jim there."

"Ned, Ned, you're not so plain-patterned as Jim."

"For God's sake, Susie," he said hoarsely and suddenly, "go away home again. It's no place for you."

Thus they had once more, as in the morning, reached the maziest confines of misunderstanding, when Bim, who had meanwhile stretched himself out between them, leapt to his feet and growled gently.

"Listen!" said Ned, his mind on the instant seeming to be swept clear of the recollection of all that had passed. A faint, inspiring sound of many hoofs came to their ears.

"It's Moltke," Ned shouted, "been horse-hunting since Saturday. H-rr-oop! Come along, Susie!" Then he pulled himself up, and said, with a mighty new elation on him, "Hear that, girl?" The rataplan of the hoofs was growing clear, and the stark note of a whip seemed to echo up amongst the very stars. "It's that, besides the queer things that we never mention, that makes new men out here. So if you stay, don't blame me if you find I'm—we're—crossed with the savage here;" and he laid aside gun and birds and plunged into the house.

The girl followed him to find Uncle Joseph already astir. Ned scattered a nod amongst the new-chums, cutting short Aunt Martha's formalities of introduction, and the whole company trooped to the front.

The cook, who had come behind Susie, with the supper things from the kitchen, plumped them

SUNDAY ON DINKINBAR

on the table and joined the group on the verandah.

A long, dim line of horses was streaming at a gallop across the level floor of the plain. In the huge vault of stillness that lay overhead and round about them, their speed was curiously magnified, and they seemed to travel to the heart-shaking, muffled thunder of their hoofs with unearthly speed. Close behind them, with his horse buried chest-deep in the dust that rose and followed like a comet tail, rode a bare-headed, dusky horseman. Now and then his right arm rose and fell; at every fall the detonation of the whip-lash sounded abroad, and was repeated in tiny volleys from the timber like the distant clapping of the hands of watching multitudes.

On the verandah no one spoke except Hulbert, who said gently to himself as he sighed luxuriously, " Oh, wee, wee, little England, look at this!"

When the galloping had ceased and the sound of the heavy rails being sent home in the slip-panel came over to announce that the horses were safe, the men went out in a body to the yards.

The women turned indoors, and the elder one began with a somewhat drawn and absent face to help the cook to lay the supper-table. Susie sat by, wrestling with her re-awakened horror of the unbleached table-cloth and the solidity of the eating accessories.

The cook paused to watch Aunt Martha suspiciously slanting a plate so that the lamplight fell upon it, and said in his tired, malicious way, "There will be sport, madam, in the yards to-morrow if Moltke's brought in the roan colt."

The feint succeeded; Aunt Martha set down the plate. "What do you mean?" she said, looking frightened.

"Oh, nothing; only Mr. Ned mentioned," he continued, seeming to taste and approve the sting of every word as it came, "that he'd sent Moltke to find the mob with the roan colt in it, or perish. He's been out six months, the colt has, and, says Mr. Ned to me, he says, ' The next man that rides that colt, Dick, will be apt to discover several new constellations, even if he doesn't find Kingdom Come.'" Dick continued his work with great nicety.

Aunt Martha stood watching him in silence, and with the look of fear deepened in her face. When Susie touched her, she started. Dick shuffled out after a final glance round of supercilious triumph.

"It's nothing, nothing; there's no danger, none at all," Aunt Martha said hastily, "in this horse-riding. I had an old uncle, a soldier that had fought in twenty fights, I suppose, and the sight of a cut finger scared him to his dying day.

SUNDAY ON DINKINBAR

We've all some silly dread that we can't outlive. The things I've been through with your uncle! and yet I'm always a baby when this buckjumping's going on. Dick knows it; and he mayn't buck at all—the colt. But you'll always notice your old aunt's a fool about wicked horses, child." She patted the girl's cheek, and smiled; but the strong face was the face of a woman watching the sea that has swallowed up her happiness.

A confusion of tongues sounded from without, dominated by the joyous chattering of Moltke, who was making up for a limited vocabulary by plentiful, descriptive grunting and a wild and liberal employment of statistics and imagery:
"Tee-day pind um blenty drack, see um foot belong that one ro'on cult——"

"You don't mean to tell me," Hulbert's eager voice cut in, "that he knows a horse simply by its hoof-prints?"

"We call 'em tracks," Uncle Joseph's voice answered; "and this nigger can swear to the track of any horse on the run, and most of the neighbours', too, as safe as if he saw the animal before him. You puzzle him, and I'll give you the one he goes wrong over. Go on, Moltke."

The boy crowed. "Kee-hee, ho'se-drack, blenty walk about, walk about; me pollow

pollow — ride — long — fife hund'd miles — h-r-r-ehee! I think it closh-up two mile."

"So much as that!" Ned put in wonderingly. "Three-quarters of a mile, maybe, eh, Moltke?"

"Yo-ai (yes); I think it dree quarts, Mis' Nédie. 'Ungry me, now."

"Run away to Dick," said Uncle Joseph. "Wait, though; look in here. Two fella missee you got um now, Moltke."

The lad followed his master to the doorway, but not beyond, and stood there, grinning hugely, and nervously fingering a battered hat.

"Why, Moltke," Aunt Martha cried, "you're splendid!"

"Pflendid me, yo-ai. You jump up like it Ole Country now, missee; 'long big fella water?"

"Ay. I bring um you shirt, too, hank'chef, my word, all same that one sky-boomerang (rainbow) you see; and look here," Mrs. Heyrick said, pointing to Susie.

Moltke grew suddenly solemn, and eyed the girl humbly with the look of an adoring dog.

"My woo-ahd! boodyerré fella White Mary. That one sit down here now — belong Mis' Nédie, I 'spect, uh?"

"There," said Uncle Joseph, smothering a laugh, "clear for the kitchen;" and Moltke, grinning again, withdrew.

CHAPTER VIII

A Buckjumping

WHEN, in the clear, still dawning of her second day on Dinkinbar, Susie was wakened by sounds of stirring in the house, and came out dressed as the first of the sunlight fell across the plain, it was to find Uncle Joseph busy and abroad, and cheerfully but firmly bent upon it that the station business was to be immediately set a-going; and that the new-chums were to be shackled without delay with the full weight of their new responsibilities.

Even as the girl emerged from her room, she was an embarrassed witness of the close of an interview between Aunt Martha and Finlay, who, being discovered by Mr. Heyrick in the act of instituting polite inquiries as to his washing, was roundly informed that he was to be his own laundryman from that day forth, and that anything in excess of the station allowance of soap would be charged to him. Then the horrified Finlay was bidden to go to the stockyards and see how horses were drafted; and he went vaguely forth.

Creswell was despatched with a bridle on his arm, along with Jim Baxter, for a first lesson in bare-backed riding, and instruction in the method of running up the working horses from the home-paddock. Aunt Martha being entirely engrossed in the business of breakfast-getting, Susie, remembering the first hour of yesterday already with something of a pang as she sought the broad-brimmed hat, made for the freedom of the open air.

To the turmoil of the milkers in the yards there was added now in another part a furious trampling and surging amongst the horses yarded overnight, whence now and then Ned's steady voice would rise from amid these new alarms. Bim and Blucher, very obsequious, but sad and preoccupied, discovered the girl and came to sit behind her, and gazed yearningly at the scene of action, like battle-hungry reserves held back from the firing line.

When Susie moved away to the stockyard, the dogs refused, with many apologies and regrets, to follow her.

As she drew closer, a climax of the mysterious trouble amongst the horses appeared to be reached. Between the lines of the rails she could

A BUCKJUMPING

see Ned, hat in hand—a single collected figure against a thronging rush of horses—winnowing the pack by wary dodging till one shining silver roan shot out of the rush by himself into a small square corner yard, where the gate was closed upon him.

Finlay was watching this stirring business in a somewhat dejected attitude from the massive top of a distant corner-post. As Susie looked, the roan caught sight of her, flung up his head, and roared defiantly in his nostrils. She fled appalled, and coasted round the fence till she reached the milking-yard, where she discovered that Aplin and Hulbert were in the charge of Dick, who, by means of a scathing commentary on their helplessness, was giving tuition in the mysteries of milking.

During breakfast, three of the new-chums seemed bewildered and depressed. Creswell alone maintained his customary air of strong complacency, and vowed he had spent a most instructive morning, though there was a faint ring of contemptuous self-assertiveness in the avowal for which Uncle Joseph had no retort but a grunt.

Aunt Martha ate little and gazed much, with the look of robbed motherhood strong in her face, at Ned, who fed stolidly, though sparingly, and spoke little. Once Susie looked up to find that his eyes, with the blue ring of the pupils showing clear between the parted lids, were set upon her face.

Something of the uncanny look she had surprised in them yesterday was there now, and in the peaked eyebrows; but something strangely mournful as well. She noticed that he endeavoured, with pitying side-glances at Aunt Martha, to stifle all Uncle Joseph's attempts to discuss the roan colt, and that, when the meal was over, and the outspoken old squatter's exuberance seemed about to get the better of him, Ned made a pretext and hurried him out.

Susie, on her father's side, came of a people that turns out warriors and horsemen, not to mention militant priests, in numbers far exceeding its home requirements; and in spite of her pity for Aunt Martha, whom she left limp and tearful in the house, race instinct drove her to the yard when the time drew near that the roan colt was to be ridden.

When she got there, Uncle Joseph was issuing stern injunctions to the new-chums, who, with the cook, the stockman, and the blackboy, were staring fixedly through the fence, as to the deadly danger of any sudden movement while the colt

A BUCKJUMPING

was being caught and saddled. He beamed in sudden delight when the girl put her hand through his arm, and came to stand beside him.

"I said she was the stuff," he muttered secretly and absently, for at that instant Ned, with a bridle in his hand, entered the narrow yard from within and quietly fastened the gate behind him.

The colt trumpeted defiance, wheeled away to the furthest corner, then faced about and stepped out springily into the centre of the yard till he stood three feet away from the man. There he stopped, his ears straining forward, his eyes, with a blue-grey sheen in them, fixed on the man's chest, while now and again he hollowed up his nostrils and blared a challenge.

His purple-silver coat shone silky in the sun; he stood there, instinct from ear-tip to hoof in every shapely line of him with all the devilry of all his unbitted ancestry; untouched by kindness; untamed by his breaking-in; fit as steel; as quick as a tiger, and, to the last limit of his lesser powers of wickedness, as unscrupulous.

In Ned's face there was a hard, grim, watchful coldness as he first, at arm's length, got his fingers on the roan's velvety nose and up along the narrow forehead, talking peacefully all the time of casual things. He was already slipping the bridle gingerly upward to the ears, and gently tickling the horse's tongue so that the bit, emblem of man's dominion, might be slid between the teeth, when Hulbert, who was in the colt's rear and in an ecstasy of admiration, moved hastily aside to get a better view. As quick as the leap of flame from a gun-muzzle the roan lifted a forefoot as high as his ears and brought it down stiff, straight, and heavy as a sledge for the man's head. Ned moved backward by the length of his foot; it was in time, and far enough, but his shirt, where it bagged above his belt, was laid open in a jagged rent by the falling hoof.

He smiled gently, and Uncle Joseph's forcibly uttered cautions saved further interruption.

The bitting and bridling, the saddling and girthing up, the making fast and safe of crupper and breastplate and surcingle on the roan colt, was a business that called for a resourcefulness and a collected courage unneeded and unknown in the tamer business when two boxers spar for an opening; for, awaiting every slightest clumsiness on the horseman's part, there lurked a lightning blow of ten-man power, on which, if he survived it, he must not retaliate. When the super-delicate work was done, the colt was let run loose about the yard with the bridle

A BUCKJUMPING

fastened to the near stirrup, in order that he might, if so disposed, waste the freshest of his anger on the empty saddle. But his wickedness was of the cooler, deadlier sort; he merely buckled himself in a few times, feeling his perfect strength, and making the leather strain and cringe, then stood in a far corner and turned his stone-coloured eyes upon his enemy.

"He means it, boy," Uncle Joseph said heartily.

"He does," Ned answered quietly, and, setting his hat firm, he led out the colt, undid the reins, and slipped the bridle over the animal's ears.

"I'm going to run away," Susie whispered suddenly in her uncle's ear. Uncle Joseph merely took a strong grip of her hand as it lay on his arm. She tugged half-heartedly at her imprisoned limb and looked about her, white-faced and cold at heart; every eye about the fence was set and strained. In the next moment the spirit of her older fathers that was in her gave thanks for that restraining hand upon her. Ned was in the saddle, with his feet home in the stirrup-irons, and the roan colt had flung loose the full torrent of his wrath.

When a horse bucks in a manner worthy of the name, it is a glorious and a fearsome thing to see. It means that one of man's oldest, fieriest, tamest servants among the brutes—having been foaled in the open forest, and run bridleless and unhandled till he has shed his milk-teeth, having tasted the sweetness of the old days of republican forest-freedom before ever the ribs of any one of his breed had been galled by the knees of human kind—has revolted, and means to fight to his last breath against all ignoble restraint of hands or leather. And when a Bush-bred colt makes war, he has all the weapons of offence at his command that through all the ages were ever wielded by any of his kin. For in him there is the wild-beast blood of the zebra, and the spring, the mettle, and endurance of the English thoroughbred.

A crimson light flared up in the colt's eyes; he gathered in his haunches, and rose. As he rose, he clipped himself with horrible swiftness into a curve till his head beneath him was buried in his own silver tail, shook himself like a wet dog as he spun about, and lighted on two fore-legs planted as stiff and straight as crowbars where the hind feet had trod when the battle started. As the shock of the alighting fore-part was delivered, the lithe hindquarters were already gathered in, and the rearing, the writhing, the swerving in air, and the plunge were repeated,

A BUCKJUMPING

this time the other way round, and re-repeated with every variation and all the ruthless tactics that strength and fury could suggest. The colt squealed and groaned in a strained, uncouth, and terrifying way; and in less than a minute dull, ragged splotches of sweat began to mar the brightness of his coat on neck and flank.

The rider, his face set like a flint, kept his eyes fixed on a point a little forward of the saddle-pommel, and held a rein clenched in each hand at quarter-length till the muscles of the forearm stood up arched and clear; though, as the horse's head was whirled beneath him, the rider's hands gave lightly lest he should be plucked headforemost from his seat. From the saddle downward he was clipped to the leather and the horse's ribs like a vice; but upward from the waist he spun and turned as if blown by the wind.

At each upward rear he gave forward; as the horse bent double beneath him he was left bolt upright upon the living arch, and his shoulders merely shook and faced about to the wrenching and swerving that looked as if it might uproot a living tree; the riving shock of landing he met sitting back a little.

After a long five minutes the bucking ceased as suddenly as it had begun, and the colt stood up, beaten in his first round, but unconquered, and champing defiantly on the bit. His forehead and nose were powdered with the dust of the stockyard, where his doubled-in head had brushed the ground beneath him. His coat was all dull and sodden, and the sweat pattered beneath him, while his nostrils spread and shrank with his heavy breathing.

The man upon him was pale and firm, and he breathed long and deep. Catching Moltke's eye, he nodded towards the slip-panel that gave from the yard into the open, and the boy ran chuckling to take down the rails.

"Going for a spin in the open, lad?" Uncle Joseph asked approvingly.

"Yes; stand clear."

The colt stepped gingerly out, and his ribs rose and fell in a mighty sigh as he looked abroad. Then he shot away for a hundred yards; at the end of that he bunched himself together once more, and for a few wild moments bucked and screamed again as he had done in the yard, ploughing up the hard earth in a circle no wider than his own length. When the spasm was over and he stood up with his nose pointed for the open plain, Ned for the first time sent his heels home resoundingly on the colt's ribs, and the roan went off at a headlong gallop, then plunged straight ahead in a series of gigantic flying bucks that carried him out of sight beyond a line of trees.

"Boys," said Uncle Joseph exultingly, "that's horsemanship."

Half an hour later, Susie was in her room, aimlessly occupied and absently idle by turns, when she saw Ned outside leading the roan colt round to the saddle-room. The horse followed submissively, looking dazed and weary.

Hulbert was walking beside Ned, looking adoringly at him and chattering blithely of his wonder at the buckjumping.

Susie's letter of yesterday, dust-covered and still wanting its commencement, was lying on the table, and an ant—this time a small black one—was exploring vigorously over and about the paper. The girl waited her opportunity, and, snatching up the sheet, she looked it over long and carefully, then tore it into fragments.

CHAPTER IX

Afternoon Tea

THE eight hundred and odd square miles of country that formed the Dinkinbar cattle-station lay about midway along the base of that great northern triangle of Australia whose apex is Cape York. Although that topmost promontory of the island is a port of call for ocean steamers, a station of imperial defence, a focus of trade, and a convenient rallying-ground for the swindlers of two hemispheres, and although along its jungle-fringed eastern coast local government and the mining speculator have brought the mixed blessings of civility, yet in its heart and along its western side there still lingers much of the mystery of unawakened earth.

All along its southern boundary the peninsula rises out of the rich, rolling, treeless, pastoral country in a line of timbered, basaltic ramparts, forbidding at first sight with their rocked-ribbed gorges and boulder-strewn earth. It needed a tough breed of men to make war on this craggy stretch and to force it into bearing. Sheep were

AFTERNOON TEA

an impossibility, for the grasses grew barbed and needle-pointed seed that clung to the fleeces and gave them all the appearance and something less than the value of so many door-mats; and the blacks were predatory in the early days, and provided by nature with ample cover. But, once established there, horses grew flat-boned, sound-hoofed, and wiry, and cattle throve and multiplied like magic on the sweet, strong grass that sprouted on the black-soiled plains, on the chocolate tablelands above the tumbled slopes, and thronged even amongst the chaos of volcanic stones. And, best of all, the scowling gullies, the reedy, meadowy uplands, and the stony stretches were threaded all about with strong, full, never-failing runnels of pure cold water that welled up plentifully from hidden springs in the black-bowelled earth, springs, it was noted—often with superstitious awe—that ran only the more plenteously in time of drought.

That wealth of water was the chief of the many saving graces of the basalt country. Year by year Mr. Heyrick would read in his newspaper of the ravages wrought by the dry times on the lordly sheep-lands not fifty miles to the south of him, of bank- and mortgage-ridden squatters, of wasted flocks, and would chuckle as he listened to the music of the water below his house and thought of his cool, high, stony land and his abundant sheltered pasturage. He was of that rugged breed that had tamed his plot of the peninsula to do his will and give him wealth sufficient to his ends; a true Briton abroad, his yeoman stubbornness widened, ennobled may be, but not weakened by the broader new-world needs; a man—as one might say whose estimate of the squatter's character had not been belittled by a too intimate contemplation—who had breathed a serener air than that of crowded England.

Something of ampler, if ruder build, there is in that fast-dying race, the old-time squatter, who has sloughed the little ways of his more recent ancestry, has freed himself by the work of his hands from snobbery and snuffling, and seems— if one sets him as a type of manhood clear of the turmoil of his daily needs—as if he might almost be some Viking of the elder days, who had laid aside his sword and shield and turned herdmaster.

But even a Viking farmer, like any other who has his living to make, must be the creature of his conditions, if he is to master them. And Uncle Joseph, on the thirteenth Sunday after the arrival of his new-chums, as he mechanically waved his folded spectacles to keep off the flies after he had absorbed the nourishing items of his weekly newspaper, was as little of the Beresark of old, and as plainly and placidly devoted to business, as any grocer.

He and his wife were sitting side by side in their old deep canvas chairs alone upon the Dinkinbar verandah.

"We'll tighten the reins on 'em to-morrow, Martha, eh?"

She was going steadily down the births, marriages, and deaths, item by item, with a forefinger, and closed the paper as she came to the last one.

"I suppose you must," she said, knitting her fingers in her lap and leaning back.

"Ay, no more of this holiday business round the head station. Give it them light at first, that's it. Makes 'em show their paces and lets one know what they're good for. It's time to make use of 'em now and begin to scrub the nonsense off them."

"Poor boys," Aunt Martha said faintly.

"Poor men," gruffly; "two of them mighty poor. But it's a fair average. There's two rank wasters in the lot, and one horseman, Martha, and one with a head."

"You mean Creswell."

"Ay, I do. By dash"—Uncle Joseph tapped

his forehead with the spectacles—" it's the hand of Providence, old woman. It'll pay. Creswell's square and sensible, and as close as wax. We'll send him south, to watch Snelling and keep his infernal cattle back. Hulbert's a rider, but"—Uncle Joseph looked round and listened, then lowered his voice—" he's a fool with his poetry and his vapourings. We'll send him north, up to the wild parts, to keep the boundary where there's no Snelling to watch—see?"

" If he doesn't turn—turn queer—Joe, the way I do think poor Ned might have done if we hadn't come back."

" And brought the girl, eh, Martha, oho?" He turned round to stroke his wife's white hair. " Nay, Hulbert's all right. He'll come in here often enough; Ned'll keep him straight. We'll make a man of him. He'd only have been a Thing at home. As for the other two——"

" I'm frightened for them, Joe. I wish they were back with their mothers."

" Their mammies!"—with deep disgust. " I declare, Martha, since that girl came, but it's as if you—you're gone that soft. Now if you hadn't me to——"

" You're just four times as big a fool about her as I am, Joe"—the tone of the retort turned it into a caress, and she pinched the big brown paw that was laid upon her knee.

AFTERNOON TEA

"Well, well. We're getting old, Martha.—But this isn't business." Uncle Joseph returned with added sternness to the question of the exploitation of his new-chums. "They can run home to their mammies, the other two, the way that ladylike nephew of mine did—Lord! if I could ha' kept him—after they've served their turn and worked out their tucker."

"If they're no good, Joe dear, send them home, and deduct their keep from that wretched hundred-pound premium you got with each of them."

Uncle Joseph sat up in his chair and adopted the manner, judicially rough, of the man who means to maintain once for all the sacredness of might against the wiles of any softer pleading.

"I tell you, Martha," he said, shaking his spectacles threateningly at the landscape, "those unlicked cubs are dear at a thousand, Snelling's price per head. They've smashed more saddlery already, and spoiled more horses, and—and made goats of themselves all round in a way that a hundred apiece won't cover."

Aunt Martha folded up the paper carefully on her knee; Uncle Joseph sat back again and continued doggedly to develop his plans.

"These two, Aplin and Finlay, will start out to morrow morning with a dray and camp fixings, and go to the south-west corner on the Meadow Flat boundary and start their dirty work, pulling the wire out of the old heifer-paddock. That's what they'll do, and it's all they're fit for."

"It's only five miles from the pub"—Aunt Martha said hastily—"the 'Three Bushes.'"

He waited for a further protest, but none came, and he went on, expanding genially as his plans took shape—"It's a Providence, Martha. If I don't wipe out that twenty-year-old grudge I've got against my aristocratic friend Snelling, may the pleuro kill every hoof of cattle on Dinkinbar."

"Still on Meadow Flat, Joe?"

"Ay, still. 'Cursed be he that removeth his neighbour's landmark.' Snelling's a rogue, Martha. He got Meadow Flat, the pick of my run—the run I found, and mighty near gave my life to keep—by a trick. Oh, but he did. You can't believe it, woman, you found him so sweet when you came, years after. He did, though. He squared the surveyor or something. You made the peace between us—it was when our baby died, God love us. But I told you it was hollow, though it's best, I know. And now my time's coming, Martha."

"Let it be, old man; we have all we need without it."

Uncle Joseph rose and made a survey of the

empty house for listeners. Then he sat down again and clenched a fist on his knee.

"There's no letting be, Martha, to a wrong like that. If I owned all Cape York Peninsula, ay, or all Queensland but that one corner, I'd fight him for it; and he knows it. I'd fought everything here from wild blacks and the wild elements to tame. bank-managers, and weathered the lot of 'em; and then Mr. Soft-sawder Snelling comes and sneaks the apple of my very eye, Meadow Flat, the cream of the run. There's no forgiveness for that, girl. If *you* hadn't come—well, I don't precisely know now how far I was from getting to work on him with the argument of the pistol-barrel. It was wilder days then."

"It's better as it is, Joe."

"Oh, it's better, ay. If I'd shot him, his heirs'd have collared Meadow Flat. Now, please God, I'll have it back before I die. He's mortgaged to the hilt; he's overstocked, and yet he's hardly a saleable beast on his run; the drought down south is driving his cattle up my way for a living; let me post Creswell down there with a boy to hunt 'em back for three months, and one fine morning I'll ride into the Bank of Ethiopia in Bingo, and make that tubby little Morrison a cash offer (thank the Lord for the bullocks sold and the new-chums, we've cash now), and Snelling'll walk out of his house and off the property he thieved with no more than the clothes on his back to call his own. That's better than shooting, hey, Martha?"

Aunt Martha was carefully smoothing out the crumpled newspaper. She had the gift of silence, and not many could have told from her passive-seeming exterior that she had tendered a conversational olive-branch which had been accepted in the light of a thistle. Fortunately, her husband was amongst the understanding ones. He relented from his stern, reproving stare upon the naked sky and plain, and applied the folded spectacles to gently rubbing his wife's uneasy hand.

"Women," he said, "are all sn—all lovers of elegance and refinement and high breeding, bless 'em. If they weren't, what sort of a ramshackle world would we get, anyhow, if a woman looked down instead of up when she came to choose the father of her children? Now, there, old girl, I'll give you charge of the case. Snelling's the nephew of a lord."

"Son," Aunt Martha said decidedly. "Not that I care."

"Oh, no; but I thought it was nephew. He's well mannered, and built like a thorough-bred, every line of him. You can't believe he's a high-class thief. No wonder. Now look at his wife."

"Yes, look at her," Aunt Martha said, quietly but firmly withdrawing her hand from beneath the caressing spectacles.

"Oh, I don't want to touch her. But she's a very fine, a very clever, handsome, cultured"—he wrenched the word out heavily—"a cultured woman, Martha."

His wife smiled a restful, superior smile.

"I'm too old for that, Joe. She's as hard as the basalt down in the creek. It's your name for her over the way she treated those new-chums, poor boys."

"Ay, ay. But she's most superior, all the same. But that's not it. Look at her niece. Now there's a girl, Martha!"

"I suppose she *is* a girl, yes," Aunt Martha said aridly, "though it's hard to believe it sometimes, what with her shirts and ties and cigarettes and things."

"Ah, but such good style, Martha. Trim and smart; a girl bound by nature to make for a high position, and to fetch her husband along with her."

Aunt Martha sat up, and in her turn seemed to take the entire landscape severely to task as she said, "Oh, yes, she'll do all that."

Uncle Joseph lay back and folded his hands, but carefully preserved his deliberative solemnity as he watched his wife.

"Very well, then," he agreed. "I give in to your likings for style, Martha. Let's be awmbeetious, as old Mac says. I'll let Snelling keep his run. We'll send Susie home—between you and me she's only a flighty thing—and fetch that Stormonth girl up to stay here, and run Ned on for a family alliance with her. Get back Meadow Flat that way, and an aristocratic connection as well. That's to your liking, eh?"

Aunt Martha had drawn herself up defiantly, and was perched on the edge of her chair.

"Well," she began explosively, and paused, as if choosing her point of attack upon this monstrous proposal.

"Well?" Uncle Joseph said serenely behind her. "It appears to me to be a most suitable notion. I'm hard on the Snelling crowd, I grant you. You stand up for 'em—for him, at least—and quite right; they're clean-bred, only they're running out for want of worldly goods. We find the goods, they fetch the breeding, and the two runs, Dinkinbar and Meadow Flat together, will make the neatest station in the Peninsula, and everybody happy."

Aunt Martha was gazing with tight-shut lips out towards the farthest line of trees. "Send my Susie away!" she muttered fragmentarily. "Fetch that—that *smart* hussy, and start my boy Ned—and that Snelling woman with her cackle, and—and cockernannies and gimcrackery"—her voice was rising as if in horror at its own recital. "Joe!" she turned at last wildly to her husband.

Uncle Joseph, with the spectacles protruding from his folded fingers, was hugging his waistbelt as he gazed at the roof, and was chuckling noiselessly. Aunt Martha broke into doubtful laughter, and raised a harmless-looking fist above him. He doubled up and cowered beneath it, holding the spectacles like a single-stick, as if to guard his head.

While the elder folk were still in this warlike attitude, Ned and Susie strolled round the corner of the house. His hands were sunk in the pockets of an ancient coat, and she, with an arm passed through one of his and her fingers interlaced, was lagging slightly and looking up at him as she talked. They stopped and regarded their elders seriously. Uncle Joseph roared to them for help.

"This man," said Aunt Martha, appealing to the younger ones as she subsided into her chair, ruffled but relieved, "is set on making my old age miserable."

"This woman," Uncle Joseph complained, pointing her out with a large thumb and forefinger, "is playing old gooseberry with my pet schemes for improving creation all round. She has no more spirit or ambition than a mussel."

"It's a very sad case," the girl said, shifting her locked fingers till they rested on Ned's arm, and looking up solemnly at him. "What is to be done?"

"I don't know," he answered, looking sternly from one to the other of the guilty pair; "it's against my principles to interfere between husband and wife. I tried it once at the 'Three Bushes,' and had to run for it. And we can't get the horse-troopers out from Bingo for anything short of murder."

Harsher methods for the healing of the domestic breach having been debated at considerable length and abandoned as impracticable and possibly unnecessarily severe, Susie, obeying an unspoken hint, occupied a share of Aunt Martha's big chair and proceeded to urge milder counsels. The men fell to the discussion of the changes that to-morrow was to bring in the working of the station.

Her few weeks of Bush life had given to the girl those ripening touches that proclaim the bloom-time of a first healthy freedom of body and limb. As she settled herself down in the chair with a nestling, natural, comfort-seeking move-

AFTERNOON TEA

ment beside the elder woman, there was in the likeness and unlikeness in contour and colour of the two a portrayal of the first and the final effects that are wrought upon home-bred women by exposure to the opener conditions of the new world. The faint brown blush of tan on the girl's cheeks and the look of breezy crispness in a loose strand of hair on her temple, were as the warm, free springtide of health that had set out upon its first stage towards the fixed and weathered tints and lines of early winter in Aunt Martha's toil-worn face and whitened hair.

There was a new comeliness—the grace of new strength from holding the bridle-rein—in the slim left hand that the girl thrust gently between Aunt Martha's fingers as they lay in her lap, spare and knotted, and so work-worn that the old plain wedding ring was half dissolved.

If the girl had grown already in strength and freedom in the Bush, she, or something, had given to the young man who leaned against the verandah-post uprightness in bearing and a trimness in his clothing that had been woefully to seek on the morning when he had found the strange white creature in the garden. The ruinous hat had given place to one of woven grass of a sailorly pattern, with a neatly pinned and folded puggaree round it; his shirt was tidy, and had all the buttons on, and he wore a necktie; coat and trousers seemed like things conscious of their own dignity and fitness, and not, as formerly, graceless grimy makeshifts for the mere covering of nakedness. The man's face denoted that he had inwardly lived up to the reformation of his vestments. A certain shiftiness of gaze — not of cunning, but of a mortal shyness and the dread of detection of uncommitted crimes—was gone, and the lost fearlessness of innocence had been almost wholly restored to the blue eyes. The beard had been trimmed, moreover—amateurishly, as the scissor-marks showed, but cunningly too.

The sounds of shuffling within the house, and of china being roughly handled, sent Mrs. Heyrick off in alarm to interpose between the cook and her best teacups, the tinkle of which she recognised with motherly intuition. Susie followed her aunt, and the men were left alone upon the verandah.

They watched the pure, hard sky in silence for a while; it was as free of any hint of moisture as a polished turquoise. Down in the southern plains the drought was eating into the flocks, and driving station-managers towards melancholy madness and station-owners down the road to bankruptcy. It was creeping north, too, this year, like a beleaguering army, and already the flanking buttresses of the basaltic tablelands were seared and desolate, and the Meadow Flat cattle were trooping northward like a routed host. As yet, Dinkinbar was snug and secure, with its shaded uplands and gorges and its gushing streams.

"Snelling's in a tight place, boy," Uncle Joseph said grimly; "and by the time we've bashed his cattle back for a month or two, it'll be too tight to fit him, I'm thinking. There's a sky like cast steel. Look at it, and the basalt creeks are running fuller than they've done this twenty years. It's war, lad, bloody war."

Ned came over and sat down in Aunt Martha's vacant chair. "War be it," he said, folding his arms; "war to the stockwhip. And Meadow Flat—the lost province—your Alsace and Lorraine, eh, Uncle Joe? Meadow Flat to the conqueror by way of indemnity. Hooray!"

"Alsace and Lor—" Uncle Joseph repeated carefully. "Oh, ah. You fog me sometimes, you brat, since you and the girl took to gettin' up these bales of books. Alsace!"—he chuckled profoundly—"good! I say, Ned."

"What?"

"I'm growing old, lad, and stiff, and mild, like seasoned whisky. It's you that'll have to comb out these new-chums, and train 'em up—or fetch 'em down, rather—the way that new-chums ought to go; down to their milk." Uncle Joseph coughed the sturdy cough that betokened his setting out upon a delicate matter.

Ned stirred somewhat uneasily in his chair. "This cat won't fight," he said firmly. "I'll help you to steady these chummies; and if the drought holds, please God you'll give Snelling his marching orders, you and Morrison between you. Then I'll shove north or west somewhere, and see if I can't peg out a run of my own."

The old squatter lay back and twiddled his thumbs fiercely. "Oh, you'll go north or west, will you?"

"Yes; it's your own plan, Uncle Joe. My little pile that you and Morrison—more power to you—made me tie up till I got my colonial experience done, that'll start a tidy cattle-run up about the head waters of the Dennis somewhere. There's lots of room there yet for a bit of pioneering."

Uncle Joseph snorted. "You're grown mighty independent, youngster."

"Oh! And I wonder who's been coming the Gospel of Independence over me these last seven years?"

The master of Dinkinbar growled savagely in his sandy beard, then suddenly relented, and laid a hand on the younger man's knee. "I did,

AFTERNOON TEA

boy," he said almost apologetically, "to stiffen your back. Barring the first year or two when there were niggers to shoot, you've had it as tough as I've had. I tried your grit by shoving you down the roughest road I could find for you, and you fetched through it. Do you suppose, you young idiot, that I was going to cocker you up all the time with notions of coming out as *my* successor at the end of your colonial experience? No dashed fear."

The elder man had unconsciously assumed the attitude and accents of a pleader, and was moving the younger one's knee gently to and fro. "You can teach the old man his business on the cattle-run now, Ned. And you've been to Melbourne with bullocks."

"Any fool can do that," said Ned. He was staring at the floor in a bewildered way and breathing deeply.

"Any idiot; Lord, yes! Any idiot can run this station better than I can myself, only I happen to want a particular brand of chuckle-head." Uncle Joseph desperately tightened his grip on the knee. "How the blazes, man, am I going to work the two runs, when I kick out Snelling, without you?" he said ferociously.

"You'll have the chummies."

"Chummies be ——" Uncle Joseph looked

behind him guiltily; then he sat up as if re-entering into possession of his lost authority, and pointed his conclusions by firmly delivering with each one a blow on the knee beside him. "You stay here; and for good. I need you; the station must have you, and your aunt would fret her heart out if you went.—And there's more than that." Uncle Joseph was patting the knee now, and looking up with transparent cunning. "You're not the breed to go away and thrash out a station for yourself, by yourself, the way I did. Nay, it's no discredit to you, boy; it's the other thing. The old woman spotted it. When we came out from home"—Uncle Joseph seemed for an instant to cast about despairingly for euphemisms, and then to fall back with relief upon his native bluntness—"when we came out from home, you had a touch of queerness on you. Eh, but you had. It's best to say it. Go a trip on the roads, and never go down to Melbourne? And the Races on? See that! And spend weeks at the out-station, not alone, but worse?"

A dire confusion had laid hold of Ned, and he made an effort to rise as he rubbed his forehead, suddenly grown wet.

"Sit down; be a man"—Uncle Joseph pushed him firmly back. "I hear the teacups—the women are coming in a minute; listen. You talk about carving a cattle-station out of the wilderness for yourself. You have the hands, sonny; you haven't the head. You'd turn hatter—and you'd do better to put a loaded pistol to your mouth and let it go, than that. Or you'd turn combo—live nigger-fashion and hate your own colour—and there's no horror in hell worse than that, for a white man. My boy, I've been near enough to it to sniff the brimstone myself; and I've seen good men go down that way, God pity 'em. Now, not another word from you or me about it—it's fixed. You're shaken, boy; turn down the brim of your hat. That's it; I'll do the talking for a minute or two. Steady now," Uncle Joseph finished in a whisper; " don't go to damnation, but stay for—Cæsar! as if I'd planned it! Look at that."

Surely all the nine Muses had conspired together to pay a surprise visit to Uncle Joseph—who was as resourceless in the planning of dramatic situations as his own beeves—in order to body forth the very essence of his thought. At that moment Susie, stepping out to the music of her own singing of an impromptu processional hymn, issued from the front door with a loaded tray balanced on her ten finger-tips as high as her own forehead. Aunt Martha followed, watching the girl with a somewhat anxious pride, and

DINKINBAR

cumbered with a large teapot held in both hands, a small folding-table under one arm, and an embroidered tea-cloth held beneath the other. "Be careful, child," she said demurely, "and catch the teapot, Joe."

Susie threw back her head and lifted the tray above it. "Caution," she said grandly, "is for fools, and the gods have our best china in their keeping. Unlimber the mahogany, aunty, while I orate a little to these men, and explain that this is an occasion."

"It is that," Uncle Joseph said gently, and with unaccustomed piety.

"Silence in the pit, please. This is the bringing in of the baked peacock, the cook's *chef d'œuvre*—translate 'chief duffer'—at the end of the old Thingumies' banquet. Kindly note my attitude. No, no, I forgot," Susie added hurriedly; "bring yourselves up to date, please, and observe, before my arms get tired, that the tableau represents 'Sunday Afternoon Tea in the Bush'; which it is the 'Assault of Civilization on the Backblocks,' or 'How the Barbarians got their Nails Trimmed.' Is the altar ready, aunty? Then down comes the Holy Grail." She lowered the tray exultingly, and began to set out the tea-things as she described the campaign she had fought that morning against Dick, before she gained a footing in the kitchen in order to bake the tea-cakes.

She had, it appeared, won possession of the fire and the camp-oven by stratagem, for she had rushed to Dick in horror to report that all the milkers' calves were loose. Having taken the citadel by fraud, she had held it by flattery, for when Dick had returned in a fury, he had found her heedless of her baking, but consumed with a desire to have her ideas put right as to what was really the ideal form of government. Dick had promptly fallen into the trap, and for a whole hour he had discoursed pithily on his pet hobby. By the time he had demonstrated the rottenness of all monarchical institutions and the villainy of all the advocates of their continuance, and had thoroughly established his vague and violent republicanism, the cakes were done to a turn.

"It was a triumph of mind over politics and other things that don't matter," Susie declared as she settled down to a frank and healthy enjoyment of her own tea. "These buns"—she eyed one of her bannocks admiringly—"are substantial, and nourishing, and homely, like big, honest Charlotte MacIver. She taught me how to make them, aunty. They're not quite so formidable, or so like military redoubts as hers, but they're having a hard time of it, all the same, to live up to the border of that table-cover."

"You'll be for hanging bunches of chintz and fal-lals round the stockyard soon," said Uncle Joseph sternly, "the rate you're going."

"Chintz!" she pulled his beard; "it's a working compromise we're going in for between—ah—between the greenhide and the chiffon states of living, just a half-way house in the way of culture, as Dinkinbar is by the road, between the styles of big, bonny Charlotte MacIver and what you call 'That Stormonth Girl,' Uncle Joe."

"Where have all the boys got to?" Uncle Joseph asked, after looking with a twinkle at his wife.

Susie began to bustle afresh, and with a heightened colour, about the tea-table.

"If I don't mistake," said Ned, "there comes one of them."

Susie looked out across the plain, shading her eyes. "It's Hulbert," she said, "and—how appropriate—! he's riding a winged horse. Broken-winged, I'm afraid, but it's certainly Pegasus."

Sure enough, wide wings were swaying at each side of Hulbert's mount as he rode up with a gun on his shoulder. As he came nearer, it was seen that at either side of his saddle was hanging an enormous wild turkey. The horse he rode, old Tearaway, had been in his day the finest stockhorse on the run; but had latterly, in his old age,

AFTERNOON TEA

and on account of his wisdom and his steadiness under gunfire, been promoted to act as turkey-horse.

Hulbert was already richly tanned, and had grown firmer and lither of body, though the undefined eagerness in his long face had become accentuated. He blushed a rich brown crimson when, in giving an account of his day, he told, with the nervous openness that is so often misread as dissimulation, that he had been over to the MacIvers'. He reddened again as if in self-accusation of betraying a comrade, after admitting absently that Creswell had ridden over to the Snellings', and that he believed Aplin and Finlay had gone to the 'Three Bushes' over some business of the forthcoming race-meeting to be held there. On each admission, Susie made a diversion to save him from his self-created awkwardness, and then appeared to repent of her impetuosity.

Still, the first taking of afternoon tea on the home model, on Dinkinbar cattle-station, was a cosy and comforting affair, and the little party, once they were launched upon the safer waters of impersonal talk, sat about the teacups till the dusk began to fall and until the cynical, superior Dick appeared and broke up the gathering with some well-directed, subtle gibes, signifying scorn of the whole affair.

CHAPTER X

Susie's Letter

"DINKINBAR STATION,
 "BINGO DISTRICT,
  "QUEENSLAND.

"MY DARLING JIM,—
"There's a kind of baronial breadth about the address, isn't there? only there's a sound in these lovely wild names up-top like the beating of tom-toms and the music of those interminable four-note songs the blacks sing round their wee fires under the big naked trees at night. You're in for it this time, my superior James, for *such* a screed! I started a *real* letter to you once before, directly I got here. That was to be the beginning of a sort of 'Diary of Impressions'—ugh! A butterfly might as well try to edit a Blue Book. I got as far as the superscription, and then, what with the awfulness of this queer, wild place at first and a huge mauve-coloured ant that came to fight me for the inkpot, and the thought of how you'd squirm

at my bad grammar and fine writing, the mind in me just went dumb and dead with *blue funk*. I tore the thing into shreds, and vowed I'd keep to formalities—and I have too—till I recovered my impudence. Now I'm better, thank you, and I'm not afraid of ants, no, nor of *snakes*, and every time your goddess of style—I'm sure she has a face as plain as a flower-pot—gets bothering me about periods and punctuation and things, I'm going to press the left thumb to my nose and extend the fingers towards her—so. And I'm going to play Donnybrook Fair amongst all the rules of grammar that I can think of. So there!

"Jim, when you told me about the Bush, and said it was all wild beasties and creepy things, and turned women into drabs and men into brutes with all the *piggyments* they had to go through, you were a little bit right and a big bit wrong. I'd call you a *Molly* if I didn't think you'd get in a rage and read no more of this, and I don't want to rob you of a treat. But you were like a man, Jimmy dear, that turns up his nose at a lovely dinner because he has fetched a microscope and keeps examining the cheese-mites under it and the dragony things in the drinking-water that eat one another, and says—the man says, not the dragon—that everything else on the table, from the soup to the sweets and the wine, must be every bit as creepy and disgusting. That sounds so wise, I'm sure it's cribbed.

"At first I believed you. You had lent me your microscope, and I saw nothing but the creepy-crawleys. Not at the very first, though, when I was in the garden on my first morning watching the dawn—people in towns forget the world's born innocent every morning—and thinking what a lovely thing it was to be alive. Then a big, hairy, touzly man came by the wall. First I nearly screamed, and then I ran for him. It was Ned, and he didn't know I was coming! And I didn't know he had come home with cattle in the night! What did he think?

"Weren't there two great men once who met for the first time and wanted to talk big and deep, and could only think of cheese or cherries or something to talk about? Well, that was us. Ned began in the most matter-of-fact way about the cows; he was going milking, and I went with him, and he introduced me to the cattle-dogs, and we let out the fowls, both of us, *outwardly*, just as if we had been round the station every morning the last seven years.

"First I thought you were right about him and that all the dirt and the hard living and the creepy-crawlies had crinkled him and dried him up right through, body and bones and heart and soul, just like his face and hands, for they *did* look scorchy. Well, so long as we talked about the old times, when we fought and sulked and loved one another turn about, it was all right. But the minute we tried to bring ourselves up to date, we found that some dour, dumb, horrible thing had come between us in these years. It wasn't always there. Sometimes when I caught him looking at me on the sly, or when he was talking in his funny, queer understanding way to the animals, he was as simple as daylight and gentler than any woman; and then I wanted to laugh and cry both together. But the next minute, if something happened suddenly, something exciting like when a cow rushed at me and when he rode the buckjumper, he——

"I *slapped* your goddess there, Jim; he looked like a man in hell. And then I felt as if all the beasts out of all my nightmares had come out in broad daylight between me and him. You may just play with your cigarette and look at your nails in that exasperating way as much as you please—I can't see you, and I don't care; but I'm like the man with the donkey's ears, I must tell some one or—bust. When Ned looked like that, I *was* in a nightmare, or it seems so when I look back at it; the nightmary beasts were crawling over him and smothering him, and he was calling out to me to help him. And I knew that if I could only rush at him and give him a good hugging and kissing, the way I used to do, that he would be all right again and like his old self. But then the beasts were holding me too, and I couldn't stir. And every time I thought of it afterwards it seemed just too silly and wild for anything; but there it was. It was all so weird—that is, in the first week or so; it's all right now—and I felt so helpless and dumb and distressed about it all that I thought the worst you had told me about the effects of the piggyness and things was quite harmless compared to the reality. Fancy how *young* I was then! I, Featherhead, thought I would come out here and *civilize* them. On the very second day after that buckjumping, which was splendid only for Ned's terrible face again while the horse was trying to throw him, I came in so horrified and heartsick and homesick that I tore up the beginnings of what was to be a nice prim, tame little letter to you, that was to have been the first of a series to tell you how nicely I was tidying everything up here, from Uncle Joseph to the cook! I seemed to wish I had been sent down to dam Niagara or something

SUSIE'S LETTER

instead, and I sat down and cried for half an hour. It was hard work, sitting there biting my handkerchief so as to make no noise, for you remember there are no ceilings here, and it felt horribly public.

"Now what has happened since then to make me quite sure that all that was nonsense? I don't know. But I *do* know that somehow you kept your attention fixed too much on the beasties and discomfortables of the Bush, and that a man—a *nice* man, mind you—is the better for 'weathering' them, as Uncle Joseph calls it. He's simpler and stronger. I know I'm cribbing this time, or going to, so I'd better own up. You remember Browning's poem that you used to rave at me for not understanding? I understand it now. I've been reading it with Ned. The Arab Doctor Karshish is so puzzled and so ashamed of his puzzlement, that the openness and happiness of poor old Lazarus seems so absurdly simple, and yet so much subtler than all the doctors' nostrums and philosophy. Lazarus is quite sure that he was raised up from the dead, and afterwards taught how to be contented with the little things about him by no other than God in the form of a certain Nazarene (who Karshish says, you remember, in a kind of 'by the way' fashion, 'perished in a tumult'). He says that of course Lazarus is mad, but he thinks it's 'very strange.' I don't, not now; but then, I haven't got a headful of prescriptions, or a professional reputation to keep up, as Karshish had, before the master that he was writing to.

"Ned, with his fearlessness and his lovely tenderness all the same for helpless things, reminds me now of a young Lazarus. Good bushmen have seen God face to face. Jim, when a gentleman gets the free flavour of the Bush about him, he becomes a rarer being, like Lazarus. You may give him a finer title by splitting up the old one. He becomes a *gentle man*. That's what Ned is, I'm quite sure.

"But how about the dumb devils in his eyes, says you? They're gone. And I've never hugged or kissed him, *not once*. Mind you, I wasn't the only one that noticed the devils. Uncle Joseph and Aunt Martha were frightened too, a little, when we came. They said he was inclined to go queer—they said it with a big Q— and that he wanted company, or else he might turn into a hatter (lovely word, means lonely-mad), and once the uncle said something about a *Combo*. The auntie seemed awfully frightened then, and looked at me and called out 'Steady, Joe,' but I don't know what it means. Now they seem to be quite happy about him, and so am I.

SUSIE'S LETTER

I often laugh over my fears now. It isn't quite right to say Ned's devils are gone, for then he would be just like anybody else. They're tamed, and all you can see of them now is that what is left of them makes him look terribly sad, somehow, as if he had lost some precious thing and was never to find it. But that's only sometimes, when I catch him suddenly round corners. Generally he's full of the quietest fun, fun that hurts nobody, the sort that doesn't get into the comic papers. You would need to see him talking to a particular pet bandy-legged kitten of his, or lecturing the cattle-dogs, or doing character-analysis of a horse, or something of that kind, to understand it. That sounds rather mad, but it's all I can tell you about it. You must have missed this most lovable phase of Ned, or did he not show it to you?

"And that brings me to my nextly. I saw the penetrating lift to your right eyebrow over these 'lovelies' and that 'lovable' of mine. 'Of course,' it said—the eyebrow said—'he's been making love to her. And she likes it.' Well, that's just what he *hasn't* done. And that's why she likes him, and sometimes hates the others, because they all *have*, or would have, if I had let them. Not on board ship, or on the way up, but as soon as I was alone here—Jim, it was awful! All except Creswell. I don't think he'll ever make love to any one unless it's *good business*. But the others, as soon as I was alone here, with no other girls about! Poor Hulbert! the yearnful way he's lain in wait for me, and the dodging I've done and the lies I've told to keep clear of him. And Aplin! I don't want to be unkind —you'll burn this—but Aplin has *terrified* me. The way he laughs, with his big jaw, and his ragged teeth, and his wee forehead. It's—I can't help it—it's so like an *ape*. One Sunday night he came home late. I was alone near the creek, and he suddenly came behind me and caught me by the wrist. I think I cried out a little, a very little. He had been drinking. What he said I hardly know. But his face! I did not know men ever looked like that, except in pictures. I told him somehow, quite gently, that he was hurting me, and he let me go. I wasn't afraid then, for I saw Ned coming up very quickly and quietly behind Aplin. I believe I began to talk nonsense very rapidly, and I went away. The men said nothing that I heard; but that night Ned brought his blankets quietly and slept outside my door. I know, because at the earliest, tiniest peep-o'-day I heard Blucher, the cattle-dog, whining there and wagging his tail against the wall, and I called him, and Ned answered, saying it was all right, and that he was just going after the horses. But his head was low down, and afterwards I saw where the edge of his blanket was pressed into a little dusty hollow in the ant-bed floor. I knew it was his, because I stitched it for him in a particular way—the way mater taught me. See what a *tracker* I'm getting! Very soon afterwards there was a new padlock and key fastened to my door and window-shutter. I wonder *who* fixed them there? Ned or I never mentioned either the sleeping or the padlocks.

"And then Finlay! He's dumb; but he's getting so dirty. It's no trouble to muzzle *his* love-making; but he will *not* wash himself or his clothes. When he lumbers up towards being sentimental, I turn the subject on washing, and he gets to work furiously for a little while with the soap, and then dies away again into dirt. What will become of him when he and Aplin go to camp alone—they are going soon—Heaven only knows. Ned was untidy and rough when we came, and stoopy, and wouldn't look you in the face for long. But I only just sewed on a few buttons and that sort of thing for him, and once I clipped his beard. Now he's quite changed.

"Uncle Joseph says this place makes young

fellows into men, if they have the makings in them. I was angry at that at first; now I'm puzzled and frightened. I thought I might have helped them a little; but there's something stronger than me that lays hold of people and makes them different, sometimes finer and gentler, but often—I'm not going to speculate, I'm trying to tell you what I see. These boys must go their way. If I put out a hand to help, it's misunderstood.

"Ned has *been* his way, a long, long way, and back; he seems to have been through a fire, and to have seen strange things. He never misunderstands *anything*, and I can trust him like a brother. I like to be near him; everything feels safe then. I love Aunt Martha—she's *motherly* to me. It's no use to try and tell how; it's good to cuddle her, and women—men too, I think—must have cuddlement or starve. But Aunt Martha isn't everything. She's the warm snuggery I can run to when I feel naughty, and rumpled, and bewildered. She comforts me, and when I'm outside the snuggery she doesn't know where I'm going sometimes. That's when she says 'child, *dear*.' Ned's bigger, but not so human to me. He's the cathedral, or the sunset, or the seashore, or the one answering string in a whole roomful of harps—the things that answer you and say nothing. I don't want to hug him now, now his queer devils have gone without chasing that way. I get quite hot sometimes when I think of the mad fits that took me the first day or two I saw him. You can't kiss the sea or the sunset, can you?

"I had to write all this headlong, Jimmy, or freeze. I don't know what's in it—it just *came*. It's taken me three days off and on while the hot fits were on me, and I won't read it over, for there isn't time. The mailman is here, and almost ready to start. I know I feel much better for writing, and you can make the most of it. I'm grown strong, and brown, and I don't care a *hang* about my complexion. I've learned to ride as if I was born to it, and I've discovered that I never lived till now, when I know what it is to feel the air singing in my ears when there's a galloping horse under me and Ned's going alongside. This is all about me, but there's a lot to follow about the neighbours, and—oh, millions of things, including Dick, our philosopher cook. The world has grown big. I hear the mailman getting ready. Write me a big letter. Try smacking the goddess, as I've done.

"Your loving sister,
"Shoozan."

'P.S.—My love to the mater."

CHAPTER XI

Colonial Experience

THE drought crept along the basaltic lands and seared first the higher ridges and then the richer, deep-soiled, lower-lying stretches of Dinkinbar, till, from the southern boundary to the bark-walled out-station in the north, the country grew desolate, and wastage of the herd began in the death here and there of weaker cattle. Drought is crueller than war, for it kills only the defenceless. The squatter has no weapons to fight against a brazen sky and an earth of iron, or has forgotten how to use them; he must sit idle, and idleness enforced, when the work of a man's best years is being undone before his eyes, is apt to breed the irritation that in a congenial subject leads on to madness.

Mr. Joseph Heyrick suffered from the irritation none the less that in his case it was little likely, even at the worst, to make for the dethronement of his stable and sturdy reason. He saw himself condemned to idleness; but all the more on that account he resolved that any opening on the cattle-run for the activity of others should be utilized to the uttermost. He set the new-chums to their appointed tasks and kept them to business, taking grim consolation in the fact that so far as in him lay he was circumventing the malignant elements, and adding considerably to the burdens of his detested neighbour to the south.

That little band of young Englishmen had been organised by Mr. Heyrick on the tightest principles, financial and domestic, for their own good and for that of Dinkinbar station; and the squatter set them to work about his run to help him through the hard time with no misgiving that their coming, and the work that he allotted to each of them, was anything but the manifestly right and proper thing for both him and them.

But there is another way of looking at the lives of young Britons who go abroad. They may go out nowadays to the curious corners of the earth, travelling hotel-wise, down buoyed and metalled roads, and may be bound, indentured, and their living, when abroad, mapped out and paid for, as in the case of the Dinkinbar new-chums. And yet they may be still—unless they go as chained oarsmen in some galley of routine of Church or State—as a pinch of downy seed unknown to botany that is cast loose upon the winds of the world. So far as parents or guardians at home can foretell as to what the new conditions are to write upon the characters of their boys, we might as well be still in the early times of Drake, when, according to popular belief, the edge of the world, or the jaws of Hell, or both, lurked behind the tempests that yelled around the Horn.

Midway along the southern boundary of Dinkinbar there lay the old heifer-paddock, some rough yards and ramshackle out-station buildings. Five miles to the east there was the Snelling homestead, and five to the westward, on the main northern road, the hostelry of the "Three Bushes." Three of the new-chums were sent to camp at the old paddock, and entrusted with the responsibilities suited, according to Mr. Heyrick's estimate, to their varying capacity. Creswell, with Moltke and Blucher to help him, was to beat back, with all undue ferocity, the Meadow Flat cattle, after drafting them gently from the Dinkinbar herd, while Aplin and Finlay were to engage in pulling out and coiling up for future use the wire from the fence of the dilapidated and abandoned paddock. Wire-pulling, even with great ends in view, is not ennobling, and Creswell's stock-keeping, though it had something of the stir of battle in it, was not being carried on under happy conditions. A warm gale of wind will brown in a single night a field of oats that was green at sundown, and shake out half the grain, ripe but wizened, before the morning. What with the sudden isolation, the unalleviated drudgery, the kiln-dried atmosphere, and the bodily and spiritual effects upon them of their daily outrage of every law of cookery and housekeeping, the new-chums, after three weeks or so, did their work on bare nerves; they were doing an early stage of their colonisation at the double, and, like the wind-blown grain, were being warped and wasted by a too rapid development.

And yet, supposing a casual visitor, full of ignorant and newspaper-fed enthusiasm for the Colonial ideal, to have been dropped down suddenly out of, say, Fleet Street, by the heifer-paddock, one might have pardoned him if he had looked about him at the broad sweep of Greater Britain before him with more complacency than was apparent in the face of the girl who was gazing out upon the dried floor of Meadow Flat. For to the untrained eye the wide landscape was full of a rousing suggestiveness.

The girl rode a silvery grey, with more than a hint about him of that matchless alloy of spirit and gentleness that is the heirloom of the Arab horse. And she did not look unworthy of her horse, so far as grace and promise of unassuming pluck were concerned. She was narrow-hipped and of a mettlesome slimness, and bore herself in the saddle as in a place that was hers by long inheritance; her clothing sat upon her as closely and as freely as the feathers on a bird, obscuring the lines of her body only to accentuate them. She shaded her steady, narrow eyes with a gauntleted hand, and looked with a long-chinned, perfectly composed, and yet supremely discontented face to right and left.

On the right Aplin and Finlay, still far off, were coming from the paddock, in Indian file, burdened with tools and shambling heavily. As they saw the horsewoman, they drew into line, squared themselves briskly, and quickened their pace.

"Idiots," the girl said gently; "frauds, staging themselves directly they see me. What are they playing now—the Budding Squatter? No, the Gentleman Navvy, strong and guileless. Yet they know I saw them last Sunday, bawling and sprawling over the bar at the 'Three Bushes'—at least, Aplin bawled."

They were both waving their hats, but she turned away without a sign.

Far to the left, Creswell, with his horse galloping and girth-deep in golden-coloured dust, was flogging viciously at the tail of a flying herd of several hundred cattle that streamed southward across the bare, timber-girt expanse of Meadow Flat, the cream of Snelling's run in the time of plenty, the Lost Province and the Promised Land of Dinkinbar. Beyond Creswell the black Moltke was flogging too, and his delighted hootings reached the girl's ears. A swirling and bellowing amongst the loitering, jaded cattle on the further flank showed where the dog was quietly at work. The white man, silent, stern, relentless, might have been a cavalryman sabreing routed infantry, and sending home death with every fall of his right arm.

"That's better," the girl said unmovingly. "Let the fight go to the strongest, for once in a way."

Creswell desisted when the flying cattle were far out across the plain, and turned homeward. The girl, without waiting for the footmen, rode out to meet him. His face was hard set and streaked with dry dust.

"I never saw the grey look better, Miss Stormonth," he said, as he saluted.

"Thank you," she returned calmly. "Send away the nigger, will you? I've a message for you."

"Moltke, scoot. And bid the cook be wary with the ortolans and the damper. A lady's coming to sup——"

"No, not while Finlay's—er—so——"

"I forgot the savoury. But we could feed in the open air, you know."

"There's not room for his atmosphere even there. No, you're going to ride with me a mile or so. Come along."

Moltke went away for the hut at a headlong gallop, standing up in his stirrups.

"You're very dirty," she said, looking Creswell over critically; "but it becomes you. There's something very like the light of battle about you somewhere."

"It *is* rather like fighting, I imagine," he answered, looking out towards the retreating cloud of dust and the spent and jogging cattle; "it helps to keep off the blues. But I'm only a mercenary, fighting other men's wars, you see; I get none of the laurels."

"Why not?"

"Eh?"

"Oh, nothing. You're ruining my poor brother-in-law's last chances in this world and the next."

"Duty, you know. And 'this indenture witnesseth' that I'm going to give Mr. Joseph Heyrick full measure of dirty work till I've done my time. And then——"

"Hey for England, I suppose?" she said sweetly.

"I don't know," he answered slowly, looking at her with a shrewd sparkle of admiration. "England's beginning to seem small; one might fall off into the water over there."

She answered carefully, as she daintily settled one of her gauntlets, " It is, it is. Then you like Mr. Heyrick very much ? "

" Immensely," he said savagely, and then seemed to toss his ill-humour aside. " There, it's a lesson. He's had me. I've got to bite on the bullet."

" But you signed with your eyes open," she said innocently.

" Maybe. Then I've lost the rose-coloured spectacles since. Oh," with desperate calmness, " it's all fair. But I wish I had been buttoned up in a tunic instead."

" Fie ! look ahead. All fair, though it's neither love nor war ? "

" What is your message ? "

" In a moment. So this big country's bitten you too ? " She was making a careful examination of her cutting whip.

He shook his fist at the steel-hard sky. " Of course, size and scope and lots of room, and all the roads open to everybody that will roll up his sleeves and isn't afraid. And look at it "—he pointed out disgustedly across the ungrassed, sun-baked plain—" isn't it the mockery of ambition? Shows a man something worth playing for, and then shrivels it up, and leaves him with his hands tied behind him."

"It may be all knee-deep in grass this day fortnight."

"Yes, somebody else's grass," he answered glumly. Then he looked across at her, and braced himself up as he looked. "I beg your pardon, Miss Stormonth."

"For letting me know that your ankle-bones are sore, not being used to chains? Don't apologise," she said. Then she pulled up, and made the fine whip chirp as she flicked it in the air. The grey reefed and sidled; she sat him superbly. "Now you must turn," she said at last. "We must not be seen together. No, it isn't propriety —that's above me. It's business; and I'm not above that."

"Horse-dealing?" he inquired; "bush-ranging?"

"No." She was carefully studying the whip again. "Stock and station, and—possibly—other agencies. This"—she waved the whip suddenly towards the coveted plain, then curved it again beneath her eyes—"all this *will*, as you say, soon be somebody else's, and not Frank's."

The last words were almost inaudible. She had the fine, steady voice of the woman of perfect health who is the implacable foe of all overt display of nerves. But in the "possibly," and in the closing *diminuendo*, there was a waver, not of weakness, but like the wind-borne note of a clear bell, that made Creswell drive his horse up close to hers. "Not Snelling's?" he asked in sudden interest.

She shook her head, and still bent to examine the whip. "You don't know the plot, then?"

"The plot!"

She nodded. "I love my brother-in-law—*immensely*"—she tried to infuse a masculine roughness into the word, but the effort ended in a delicious throatiness—"and my sister as—as only women, especially sisters, really know how to adore."

"I believe they *can* hate. Well?"

"I've heard so. Look!" she raised her head, closed two wonderful rows of teeth on the whip, and shook her head wickedly. "Well, Frank's been hanging on the selvedge of ruin these five years. He's a gambler. All the Rainscourts are. And all the Stormonths are fools."

She prolonged the word in a delicate upward inflection of inquiry. Creswell cleared his throat formally.

"Thank you," she said, and laughed in the manner of women whose affections do not go out unguided by a sense of expediency; "all but one. That was neat of you. Well, here it is. Half my dow—my patrimony's gone into the bottomless pit of Frank's affairs. Now they're besieging me for the other half, to throw after the first."

"Well, well?"

"Well, that only means, at the best, giving Frank a little longer time to spell R-u-i-n. I might run away. Somehow—England is damp, and small, as you say—I prefer to fight." She made the whip sing in the air again.

"Go on," he said, filling and squaring his chest.

"These Bush houses make eavesdropping compulsory. I heard it in the small hours this morning. Frank had been to Bingo to see Morrison, head of the Bank of Ethiopia. Morrison must have his pound of flesh. Frank hasn't an ounce to give; but he said—I heard him—that my little pile would be a small steak to go on with. Clever, wasn't it?"

"Very, and most brotherly."

"Brother-in-lawly. They've nearly killed me with kindness to-day, and I'm grateful accordingly. And now Frank has a fortnight to pay what Morrison asks, or——" She paused.

"Or what?" he asked fiercely, and came closer to her.

She spoke very quietly, looking above his head. "Or see the roof sold above him, and the run go from him and his heirs for ever at a fourth of its value, for what he's borrowed on it. And there's the drought, and he has no cattle to sell; and there's *you*, my warlike friend"—she suddenly pointed the whip at his chest, looking at him keenly above it—" hunting his cattle back to starvation."

" But who'll buy the——" he said dazedly, and stopped.

She fell to examining her whip again, more closely this time, for the dusk was drawing in. "Why," she said demurely, " Mr. Joseph Heyrick, of course, unless—er—somebody else. It's an old grudge of Mr. Heyrick's against Frank that he got Meadow Flat by a trick. Morrison expects the offer from Dinkinbar any day, and he'll take it, unless the money is paid within two weeks. Three days are gone already. You're a pawn, Mr. Creswell, in the game, or a knight, rather—a knight of the pigskin—laid on to harass my poor brother-in-law in his extremity."

He gave his horse's ribs a sounding thump with his open hand, and then sat high in his saddle, looking down at her bent head. He seemed like a man re-moulded, or as one turned from clay to steel, since his meeting with her half an hour ago. A hand that he had raised towards her was diverted on its way, and went to stroke his young beard gently. He was five-and-twenty, and filled with the sublime restlessness of his world-striding race; and the woman had come to make order and plain day of the blackness he had seen a moment ago in his future.

Nevertheless, he merely said, with the elaborate carelessness that overlies the business manner of the born maker of bargains, "What is the weight of this pound of flesh, I wonder?"

"Five thousand," she said, in as matter-of-fact a voice as his own.

"Oh! I have but three in this world, or else I shouldn't have minded. However——"

"I," she said very calmly, "have still two."

They looked long at one another in the deepening twilight. "A man," he said carefully, "in this country, with a head, and hands, and some one to——" Something in her manner checked him. "I could give you a hold on the station for security."

She gave a toss, and made a small sound of anger.

"Plain business then," he said downrightly. "Can you meet me in Bingo to-morrow afternoon?" She nodded quickly several times.

"Hands on it, then." He held out one of his. She hesitated, and finally laid the point of her whip in his palm. He clutched it, and began to draw it gently to him. For the first time she seemed to melt a little, and gave weakly towards him; but the next instant she plucked the whip free and spurred the grey several yards from him.

COLONIAL EXPERIENCE

"Go back to your supper," she called. "If you move a step I'll—I'll throw myself into the arms of the enemy. It's till to-morrow only."

"What about your message?" he shouted after her.

She sang over her shoulder, full and clear, a musical phrase without words, except on the last three notes, which she drew out melodiously on the syllables "A St-a-a-tion." Then she cantered away, laughing joyfully.

Creswell stretched both arms high above his head and watched the stars mustering in the sky until long after the sound of the grey's hoofs had died away. Then he turned back, whistling the snatch of music intently over and over again, as if searching for the right words, which had been parted from the notes in the lumber-room of his recollections.

When he reached the camp, it appeared that his search had been successful, for he was singing at the full pitch of lungs and voice :—

Faint heart ne-ver won fair Lay-day.

"No, it's only dam cheek like yours that wins," a muffled voice retorted. It was Aplin's, and he was lying face down upon the bare earth before the hut, with his forehead resting on folded arms. Finlay sat on the ground hugging his shins, a rumpled, unsavoury figure.

Aplin, without raising his head, wandered off into a wild discourse; he almost sobbed with rage at Finlay's unguarded manner of sucking a hollow tooth; he laughed in a tragic way as he stumbled on the recollection of Sunday's carouse at the "Three Bushes." When Finlay cut in vacantly, saying that a cake sent out from the homestead had been wrapped in a sheet of the *Standard* containing a list of all the London theatres and their plays, Aplin groaned, "O God!"

Creswell, as he went to hunt within the hut for supper, flipped the prostrate Aplin with a strap. Aplin scrambled to his feet with a growl, and drew back a doubled fist.

"There," Creswell said, facing the other, but not lifting a finger; "I'm sorry, old chap. Fact is, we've all a touch of the dry-rot. Want shaking up."

Aplin laughed hysterically and turned away. "I must rush and have a wash and a change," Finlay said briskly, and hurried off with towel and soap. But when he reached the creek side, he sat down aimlessly and flicked his towel at the black water. "What's the use?" he said. "It looks so beastly cold"; and he returned to the hut unclean.

CHAPTER XII

Where Races Meet

ON the northern confines of Dinkinbar, also, woman and the weather were joining their wayward, incomputable strength to defeat the squatter's simple ends.

Sydney Hulbert had been a "difficult" child and an "impossible" young man, according to those who had been most fully empowered to misgovern him—his parents. He had expended the strength of his infancy on the little wasting wars called fits of temper; his schooldays had been passed in self-upbraidings for lessons unlearned, the brief exaltation that goes with fitful, empty enthusiasm and spasms of heady bravery, and the unspeakable protracted misery that follows after it. By three-and-twenty he was still uncentred, vaguely bent upon Art and the despair of a commercial father and a mother of suburban mind, when chance swept him into the net of Mr. Joseph Heyrick, and to the antipodes, to the intense joy of himself and, after the parting wrench, to the relief of his parents.

DINKINBAR

On the station, after his over-anxiety to learn new things had ceased to confound him, he developed a curious serenity under the eyes of others, and that mute tactfulness amongst animals that marks the born stockrider, which delighted Mr. Heyrick, and caused Hulbert to be promoted to the charge of the northern out-station. He was earnestly warned against "worrying," exhorted to come to the homestead every Sunday, or oftener if he chose, and to cultivate the acquaintance of the telegraph man at the repeating station. Ned Baxter, the stockman, put him in the way of filling his new office.

After three weeks he had been twice to the head station, and on each occasion he had been in wild spirits. He rode after his second visit up the little valley that led to the out-station as the sun sank behind the trees. The runnel of clear water still hurried down between its edges, like liquid gold in the colour of the sunset, and gave a point and finish to the picture of dearth that lay about it. It made a fine mockery of pouring out boundless wealth in a land where there was no food to buy. The plain was bare and black, except for filmy, sickly patches of dead grass that the cattle had gnawed to the roots, and the ground had opened into rifts wide enough to take a horse's hoof. The ridges were tufted here and there with hard wisps of stubble, as eatable and nourishing as so many bunches of copper wire. A draggled procession of cattle, all lank and weary-footed, was filing into water, but showing no heart when they reached it to drink full-throatedly. They dipped their muzzles forlornly, and bellowed to one another between-whiles in starved notes, each note a song of famine.

For a fortnight Hulbert's work had consisted in dragging out, by means of a draught-horse and chains, weak cattle where they had foundered in the boggy edges of the creeks. It was labour as cheerful as hauling drowned bodies from the sea, with the risk, in the young stockman's case, of subsequent horning and trampling superadded; for in the rescue of the cattle the extremes of brute perversity were revealed. The beasts, when their feet were fettered by the black mud, appealed to him for help in their extremity with shuddering flanks and pitiful moanings, and unfathomable yearning in their eyes, that made him sob; but, once he had put the chain about their horns and hauled them out, some curious mixture of fear, distress, and thanklessness overcame them, and they devoted the first moments of their restored liberty to charging him. Generally weakness rendered these attacks harmless; but often it needed more than a little of the courage and quickness of the bull-fighter to keep hold and pull on the thong attached to the chain so as to free it from the beast's horns. This rescue-work is the kind of station business that, undertaken by two or more, falls under the head of novelty and is conducted in a spirit of emulative horse-play; but, carried on alone by such a one as Hulbert, susceptible as he was to that strictured, dumb uneasiness that goes abroad in drought-time, it was the sorest aggravation of his solitude. And solitude is a corroding poison to such as he. But the fears of the women at the station for him in his loneliness were disarmed, if not allayed, by his hilarity when he came in on Sunday. Mr. Heyrick pointed to him, brown, lean, and wiry, as the living fulfilment of his prophecy. Hulbert was being made a man.

All the way out from the homestead the horse, listless and weak from under-feeding, had bored incessantly to the off-side most maddeningly. By the time he reached the solitary out-station, Hulbert was in a white heat of irritation, and as vaguely woful as he had been insanely high-spirited at the homestead.

"Most merciful Providence," he said bitterly, as he looked along the desolation of the flat, "no cattle bogged to-day." All the beasts stood round drearily and perfectly still, and watched him like so many retainers defrauded by him of their just rights. He pulled up in the midst of a crowd of them, and looked from one to another. Then he dropped the reins on the horse's neck and looked up, holding his clenched hands towards the sky and shaking them with every sentence as he spoke.

"What is it to me? It's not my land—not my cattle. I might go in to-morrow and tell them this is driving me mad. I can't; I go and play the fool instead. Something's withering up the heart in me. It's this awful land, where the rivers die out in deserts and never reach the sea. It's the drought. O God, O God, send rain upon the earth. There's mist and the smell of autumn in England now. And music. And London's roaring. Christ, be merciful."

He looked round him; the cattle were staring foolishly. The horse bored off heavily and stupidly in the wrong direction. Hulbert raised a switch in his hand and struck viciously at its head; the poor brute swerved blindly; Hulbert jumped down, put his arms round its neck, and groaned. One of its eyes was closed where he had struck, and a tear rolled down from it. He led it to the hut, unsaddled it gently, and rubbed its ears tenderly before he turned it loose.

He bolted his hard, hot supper ravenously, but without appetite, and smoked furiously for a little while as he sat upon a bench outside the door of the hut. But the dead, vast silence drove him within, and he fastened up door and window-shutter feverishly, like one expecting an attack. He lighted the broad wick—a strip of moleskin trouser-leg—of the fat-lamp; tried to read a weeks-old, limp rag of newspaper, and flung it away; tried whip-plaiting, and found himself staring into the smoky flame while the sweat of a nameless fear ran upon his forehead. The faceless imps of solitude had charge of him; he was unmanned.

A naked hand was swept over the sheet of bark that did duty for a door. The sudden, definite call of danger braced the man inside as a tang of sea-breeze striking through murky, fog-blinded city air might quicken the blood; he blew out the light, and crouched silently within reach of the door.

To his eyes it was pitchy dark within the hut, and silent everywhere but for the sound of his own racing heart. His revolver was at the homestead, snug in its immaculate holster, buried beneath the weight of his " colonial outfit " of things that were starkly useless once they had crossed the London shop-counter. His hankering after deeds of arms, to be done against yelling, cattle-raiding, uncouthly-weaponed savages, had been ruthlessly trodden out under the iron heel of Mr. Heyrick's deadly downrightness; one straight shot, fired fifteen years ago, had quit the station of nigger-hunting for evermore. Nevertheless, a human hand, and assuredly no white man's hand, had come suddenly, out of nowhere and the night, to fumble at the latch. That brushing of the door spoke danger to the man inside; and the alarm, being real, and wrought by a thing of bones and blood, even though there might be death behind it, was unspeakably welcome after the dread of unhuman things that had gone before.

Hulbert stooped so long that his knees began to ache, and his heart settled to a strong and steady beat, and still the silence was unbroken. He had seen some ragged leavings, bones and rotting scraps of clothing and collapsed hutches made of boughs, down by the creek, where blacks had recently been camping; but about the station he had noticed a curious reticence concerning them. And the telegraph operator—for whom Hulbert had conceived a deadly loathing, chiefly on account of his manner of exploring his wisdom teeth with a forefinger—had said that all non-working blacks had been warned to set foot upon

Dinkinbar no more, and had appended vulgar hints as to the reason which had intensified Hulbert's detestation of him.

"What name you, stop insi'?" It was the voice of a girl at the door. Hulbert rose to his feet, and smiled radiantly to himself in the darkness.

An open palm and outspread fingers began to beat lightly and irregularly on the door, and the little voice broke from beseeching into sobs. Hulbert merely stayed to look about him in the black darkness like a man wakened suddenly in a strange place, then softly undid the door. It was no sooner opened than two arms were round his shoulders, and a girl's face was snuggling against his neck. She was black, but warm and body-sweet, and utterly human.

For some moments she sobbed and laughed with her face hidden; then she knit her hands behind the man's neck and looked up at him rapturously. But when she saw his face, she pushed him from her, so that he staggered into the hut, and she herself ran backward, crying out like a wounded thing. He reeled forward, and made to follow blindly after her, but as he passed the doorway he put out a hand and gripped the post so firmly that the whole slender framework of the hut shook as he was checked. He turned back angrily, as if to cast off a restraining hand upon him, and wheeled to run out again. The girl was gone. "Come," he said, as if to the hindering cause, "maybe you're right"; and he caught firm hold of the door-post again. But he called up the dark ridge, "Who are you?"

"Noorna. Where Nédie?"

"Come here."

"No. Where Nédie?"

He ran out, and called again; there was a small sound of falling earth, and the voice answered, from a greater distance than before. He followed it, and again it moved away.

It was in the dread waste and deepest darkness of the early hours that Hulbert returned to the hut and leaned himself, dead-beaten with fatigue, in the doorway. The heavens were throbbing and ablaze with a numberless profusion of stars, that yet shone with a lifeless fervour infinitely remote, as though their light had been withdrawn from the world to make way for the advent of the living dawn.

The young man turned inside and absently dug amongst the ashes in the fireplace for glowing embers; he laid twigs on the red coals, and fanned them to a blaze with his hat. He blinked and yawned as the light flared, then subsided to the earthen floor and sat with a foot on either side of the ashes, and sunk his chin between his hollowed hands.

"I'm grown old this night," he soliloquised. "Should hardly have wondered, I've been away so long and so far, if I'd found a hotel here when I came back, all ablaze with electric light, and a station on the Trans-Continental Railway to Cape York, and Albert Edward King, and Parliament moved to Exeter Hall. Ha! I've been long in the wilderness.—If I had the words! But wisdom's dumb; and books to the libraries are dust unto dust. All the shades of life are mixed from precious few primary colours. Red, yellow, blue. Sleep, sex, sweat. Should I have run out? It was madness either way, and folly both. It was a case of tug-o'-war between flesh and spirit, and I stood by to see. Who won? Bothered if I know. Think the rope broke. What did I tell her when I started out on that wild hunt? Don't know. I do know the *Ritt der Walküren* was a tame affair beside it. Where has she gone—to the station?" He looked up with a touch of his old restlessness, but subsided into good-humoured lethargy again.

"Can't say." His eyelids were lifting and lowering sleepily. "The God that guides battles and sees the sparrow's fall—no doubt has—eye

upon us. Certain I'm talking high-class philos—
'phy. Been heart—'v—things. Cobwebs."

He dragged himself to his feet from a sleepy
lurch over the fire, and pawed his way drunkenly
to the door. A stain of whiteness, so dim that
the faintest drift of star-mist seemed shaped and
clear beside it, was showing in the east. An
invisible wagtail close at hand—earliest of early
birds in the Bush—shook out his shrill, precise
"Tweedle-deedle-deedle-deet-tweet-chuck."

"The day is at hand," Hulbert said as he reeled
to his bunk. "And the commonplace. Wonder
is my hair white?"

It was on the day that Susie Thynne's long
letter had been committed to the mail-bag, and
she stood to watch the mailman, his weary hack
and his loaded pack-horse, go shambling away.
She watched them till her eyes ached, and until
man and horses dwindled shimmering down the
plain; they seemed to dissolve in the liquid heat
as sugar-crystals melt in water.

As the mail-carrier and his horses slid behind
a belt of trees, all three of them executing apparently a last weird fandango before they should
finally dislimn and be absorbed into the heat-
racked air, a sudden passion of home-sickness and
a vague distress shook the girl's heart, and she

reached forth her hands and almost cried out to the disappearing horseman. The unpitying sky and the exhausted earth were eloquent of desolation, and seemed, now that her letter was gone—without any word of them—to be full of grim forebodings. The girl was suffering in a fit of that unrest that is apt to follow in the mercurially-minded after the cheery but unsatisfying abandonment to a heady discursiveness; and in the relapse the utter sterility of the scene before her gibed at all hopefulness and gaiety, till her departed letter took the colour of elaborate self-libelling and a childish distortion of the truth.

A limping creature was skirting the creek-side beyond the stockyard, and the girl watched it from the verandah, first in fear, then in pitying curiosity. It was the only moving thing visible, and its wounded, weary progress amongst the she-oaks was rendered doubly arresting to her by reason of the distorting sun-haze. There was a tragic liveliness imparted to the creature's limbs that was cruelly discordant, as though a funeral procession passing in the street should, being seen through faulty window-glass, seem to cut boneless, impossible capers, and indulge in weird, inhuman pantomine.

The little weary figure leaned itself up at last against a tree and looked towards the house. It was a black girl, and plainly she was spent with fatigue. But when she caught sight of the figure on the verandah, she suddenly turned and dodged like a tired sharpshooter from tree to tree, and disappeared below the bank of the creek.

The creature might need help, or it might be that she had been set to spy out the nakedness of the homestead against a night attack by savages. In any case, the episode tasted of adventure, and came as a timely intrusion into Susie's fit of despondency. She seized her hat and ran full speed, and tingling with agreeable suspense, for the point where the black girl had disappeared.

Mrs. Heyrick, having done all the work that her hands could find to do, was seeking comfort in the Scriptures against the uneasiness that was abroad. Hearing a well-known footstep, she looked up with the smile she had always ready for Susie Thynne, but it died out when she saw the girl, who had come to stand in the doorway, where she swung herself back and forwards on her outstretched hands, looking hard above her aunt's head.

"My child, what has happened?"
"Nothing; oh, nothing."
Mrs. Heyrick held out two shaking hands; the Bible fell from her knee with a thud. "Come

here, quick, child, here to my arms, and tell me."

"I will not come to you. I can tell you nothing you don't know already. If you had told *me*. But I have had my 'colonial experience' now." She laughed loudly. "My education's finished. I may go."

She turned away, and before the elder woman could overtake her she had bolted herself in her bedroom. She made no sound in answer to Mrs. Heyrick's tearful appeals at the door.

CHAPTER XIII

In Time of Drought

THE night lay still on Dinkinbar, and hot—so hot that the very moonlight fell at first upon the earth with a sultry flare, for the moon rose sluggishly, and showed a featureless, gigantic disc that seemed as though it must have issued from the jaws of some huge furnace that lay beyond the hills. The shadows started out and lay full length and dusky red across the plain, making the heat visible.

Mrs. Heyrick lay back in a deep canvas chair, showing a distress of weariness in every limb and line, and flicking restlessly now and then at her face with the corner of a sodden handkerchief. Light footsteps were going uneasily to and fro from room to room in the empty house. As they came out and paused upon the threshold of the front door, the grey-haired woman shrank a little in her chair and then lay still, but neither turned nor spoke.

"You think I'm quite right then, Aunt Martha, to go away back home at once after this?"

"Susie! did I say that?"

"No, you didn't. That's just it. You bring me out here—why did you bring me here, I wonder?—and just the very first real trouble that turns up you refuse me your help and sympathy."

The elder woman swayed her head wearicdly against the chair and swallowed a sob. "Come here to me, child"—she made room beside her and held out a hand—"come here and try me. Don't speak of it while it's hot in you, and on a night like this. I know how it tries the nerves, this weather. Sleep on it, Susie."

"Sleep!" The girl laughed derisively, and, leaning a hand on each door-post, looked straight before her. "The weather has nothing whatever to do with it. I won't come near you; and it's just the time to speak plainly about everything. No, sit where you are, Aunt Martha. I tell you I mean to talk the whole matter calmly out, and if you rise, I'll run away."

The elder woman was crying noiselessly, and making no attempt to wipe away her tears; the younger stared out movelessly across the plain. "You might at least have warned me," she said at last with a hard fretfulness.

"My dear, I didn't know," Aunt Martha said weakly and faintly. "I'm old and dull, and you

IN TIME OF DROUGHT

—you're fine and quick, and—your young eyes see what I've missed. It's you that's teaching me new things."

The girl flung aside the offer of submission with an angry toss. "You've lived your life here, and watched one man sink lower than a savage—if he or I had only died!—and helped to set four more in the same way of going, and you sit by and see nothing—nothing. Ha! ha! You didn't notice either, did you, Aunt Martha, that they're doing your work all the time—making you and Uncle Joseph rich?"

Aunt Martha, her face buried in her hands, was rocking woefully to and fro in her chair.

"Child, be still, be still!" she moaned; "you'll break my old heart."

"No, oh no"—the girl was swaying herself gently with her outstretched hands—"hearts do not break. And what does it matter, any way? Nothing; nothing at all. God makes them to wear well—too well. Now I know what it means to be a man. Courage and gentleness and truth and courtesy are nothing. They're sins—out here they are, anyhow. He must take them all—all the nobler things in him—in both hands, and stamp the life out of them, and fling them to the dogs—no, to the blacks. Then he'll get on in the world."

Aunt Martha threw herself back limply in the chair, and moaned.

"Then he'll get on. And the woman's part is to sit by with folded hands and see nothing, and say nothing, and do nothing till he's a finished brute. Then she gives him her body, and they order her—her shroud it should be called, and there are wedding bells."

"Hush, dearie! Hush, my lamb, for the love of God!"

Susie laughed. "Yes, for the love of God, for it isn't the love of woman." The white figure with the arms outspread continued to sway rhythmically in the doorway.

The moon by now was above the fiery vapour-belt that lay about the earth, and her light upon the plain was hard and clear. Two riders, their horses plodding dejectedly, were approaching the house.

Aunt Martha rose hurriedly, and laid a hand on Susie's arm. "There, my pretty," she said gently; "come with me now, and you'll see the old woman knows your sorrow. Come. It's bitter times. See the men, how tired they look. Come away."

But the girl's hands clung obstinately to the door-posts, and the muscles of her arms were rigid. She paid no heed to Aunt Martha's pleadings, and the men came slowly and silently forward. They rode heedlessly, and would have passed the house in silence had not Susie, unmoved by Aunt Martha's timid beseechings, hailed Uncle Joseph as he passed. Both men pulled up, and peered inquiringly into the dimness beneath the verandah.

"Oh, it's only a little thing," Susie called in a ringing voice as she still, unhindered by Aunt Martha's hands upon her, swung herself monotonously in the doorway; "a matter of no consequence, none at all. I'm going home." The voice began to wander strangely amongst tones that were strident and unfamiliar to it. "My aunt and I have—we are quite agreed—talked it over quietly. I only mention it — because it's quite settled, and we won't—refer to it again. Thank you, because—the cause—the cause of my—the cause——"

Aunt Martha was moving aimlessly and in an agony of helplessness about the girl, who swayed gently as before. The men had dismounted silently. A pause followed on Susie's words, a pause into which there broke the faint, incessant voice of the river below as it muttered and babbled between its drought-bitten banks.

The people about the verandah were so still when the girl's voice had faltered and ceased that the sounds of three dragging steps and then of a heavy double plunge in the deep water-hole below the house fell like a blow upon their ears.

"Fetch a light!" Ned shouted, as he raced down the slope. Uncle Joseph followed more carefully, gathering twigs and leaves as he went, and the women were left alone. The horses moved spiritlessly about, getting their feet entangled in the hanging reins.

When the noise of Ned's hurrying down the bank ended in a sullen splash in the creek, the girl stood up still; when the tree-trunks on the bank were patterned against the blinking of a fire-glow down by the water, she started suddenly at an unsteady run for the light, leaving Aunt Martha to follow her, beseeching desperately and unavailingly.

When the women reached the water, Uncle Joseph was feeding a wood fire, and Ned, bareheaded, his clothes clinging to him and the water squelching in his boots, was stooping and peering along the line of the steep, black, muddy margin with a swift, silent, savage intentness in every step and movement that betokened a business of life and death. Crouching suddenly lower, he shot out a finger, as if proclaiming that what he sought had been found. He rose to his fullest height, joined his hands above his head, and with one look upward he dived and disappeared into the black water.

The song of the shallows above the pool stole down like music on the heavy air; the broken surface was marred with fleeting, tawny flashes, like wisps of flame from a wind-blown torch, and a dying, drowsy "glug-glug-glug" sounded as the water lipped beneath a hollow in the bank. The three figures by the fire neither moved nor spoke, and but for the shifting sparkles in their eyes they appeared as steady in the leaping light of the fire as the very tree-trunks round them. The common laws of life seemed for some incalculable time to be suspended for them, until the surface of the water was troubled from below and a head rose; then a pair of arms and shoulders, labouring heavily towards the bank with a limp and lifeless burden.

Uncle Joseph planted himself on the slope within reach of the water, and reached back a hand and arm which the women seized from above, leaning their weight upon it as he caught a wisp of the mass of black hair that was floating and clinging idly round Ned's neck and arms. Then amongst them the three, without a word except of hard-breathed instruction to one another, drew out the wet, round-limbed body of little Noorna, the black girl. It was naked, save for a wisp of sodden rag that was tied about the waist, with its ends firmly knotted round a stone twice as big as the girl's head.

Ned drew himself painfully, like a spent and wounded animal, on hands and knees up to the bank and crouched at the feet of Noorna, at whom he stared dazedly, while his body, incapable of further effort, heaved and sank to his deep and broken breathing. The old squatter and his wife fell at once, with the firm despatch of folk that are seasoned to alarms, to restorative measures on the body of the girl, while Susie, overcome with a curious stillness of demeanour, helped in the work of mercy as she was bidden, firmly and capably, but coldly, and as if there were neither heart nor hope in her endeavours.

In half an hour Uncle Joseph stood up, abandoning his efforts at resuscitation as promptly as he had begun them. "She's dead," he said dryly, wiping his wet forehead. "The savages are wiser than us in these things, and braver. They never half do it. Close down the child's eyes, Martha. She must be buried by sunrise."

Aunt Martha knelt beside the body and closed the staring eyes and composed the limbs, already stiffening. Susie looked on a moment, then suddenly knelt down opposite her aunt and helped tenderly and patiently in the work.

IN TIME OF DROUGHT

Uncle Joseph made as if to draw her back, but his wife held up a hand against him. "Leave her, Joe," she said quietly; "it's the woman's share."

They crossed the hands upon the breast, and tidied up the wild black hair, and so ordered the little body that in the red light of the waning fire it lay as if asleep. When the work was done, the two white women knelt upright a moment, with hands on knees, looking down upon the black one. Ned was standing up by Noorna's feet now, with muddy hands and clothes, numbed and frightened-looking. Uncle Joseph silently uncovered, and for a moment the chattering of the water at the creek-crossing filled all the air with its sound.

"There," Uncle Joseph said, replacing his hat; "come, this is no time for talking."

He laid his hand almost roughly on Susie's shoulder, for the girl had flung herself down beside Noorna, and, after kissing the cheek, was whispering wildly in the dead ear. Ned, as he stooped forward and caught the girl's words as they fell clearly on the stillness, was agitated as if invisible hands were shaking him.

"Martha," Uncle Joseph called sternly, "take her away."

But the girl was unmoved by touch or appeal,

and continued her restless whispering, clasping Noorna's face with one arm. Except the first few words that had set Ned shaking, none heard what she said, for Uncle Joseph kept on issuing his peremptory commands so as to drown the girl's words in his.

At last she came hurriedly to her feet, and stood facing the shivering Ned. At sight of him she threw out her hands repeatedly, and with averted face seemed for one wild instant to fight against crowding horrors. Then she dropped senseless beside the body of Noorna.

CHAPTER XIV

God Sent His Messenger

THE master of Dinkinbar paced in the dead of night on stockinged feet along his front verandah. The iron above him sang to the steady lash of straight-falling solid rain; and rain plashed from the hollows of the roof to the ground below, sending up a minute babble like the voices of children. The air was moisture-laden and sweet to the mouth; from out of doors there came from the whole earth a soft, huge sighing like the breath of a sleeper that has sunk from fever-tossing into cool, life-giving, dreamless rest; and from the broad face of the plain, lost in darkness, there rose the gruff thanksgivings of a multitude of bull-mouthed frogs.

The music of the pastoral hymn of praise for mercy long withheld that rose on every side of him seemed merely to add poignancy to the unaccustomed troubles that had been laid upon the squatter, closing his lips to thankfulness for the ransom of his possessions. At one end of the verandah he stopped at every turn before a dim-lighted, curtained window that shone like a sleepless eye in the darkness of the house-front. There had for long been stillness behind the curtain, and the faint, distressing fragrance of a sick room hung about the window; and each time as he paused before it Mr. Heyrick bent to listen eagerly. But at the other limit of his walk he would often stop and give a double-handed twist to a paper he held clutched behind him, and stare out ferociously into the rainy darkness. More than once he drew a hard breath as if to curse the very sound of the rain; then the silent room would draw him back again to listen.

He was wringing the paper in his hands when a whisper called him to the doorway, and he hurried to it. His wife was there. She put a hand on each of his shoulders and her face against his breast, and broke into quick and smothered sobbing. He dropped the twisted paper, half carried her to a chair furthest from the sick-room, and sat down beside her, bowed and broken-looking, and staring out stupidly before him, with one arm about his wife's shoulders.

Mrs. Heyrick tried again and again to speak; but her voice refused control. At last she con-

GOD SENT HIS MESSENGER

trived to whisper in snatches, choking wildly between them,—

"She's — cool — and quiet. Sleeping like a baby. The rain—the rain saved her. She will —be well."

Mr. Heyrick straightened himself up at the words and held in a mighty breath, looking wonderingly at the roof above him, and rocking his wife slowly in her chair with his big hand. "God bless us all!" he said gently, letting his chest subside on the words.

"You thought—the worst. I could see it. I couldn't tell you—couldn't speak. It's my own— body and mind lying there. Wherever she went —I was going too. The poor wounded thing. My heart's blood is in her."

"There, there," he said, stroking the grey hair gently.

"Joe," she said, drawing down the hand from her head, and holding it fast in both her own, "what is the life she's come back to? It was death to lose her, but—oh, my lamb, my lamb,— what's left for you?" She lay back and locked her fingers tighter on the hand in her lap. "I brought it on her; I"—she moaned,—"I brought her to her sorrow. If I hadn't urged her to come!"

"See now, see now; there's sorrow everywhere; and at home there'd have been none to share it with her, as you can share it. It's a dark hour o' the night, and maybe joy cometh in the morning. We wore through a blacker night than this, Martha; and even for that there was comfort."

The fingers tightened again suddenly on his, and then relaxed; and for a long while they sat silent.

The wide-throated frogs kept up their tumult incessantly, and, though the noise roared in the ears as loudly as the beating of countless hammers near at hand, the hubbub fell agreeably on the senses, and accentuated rather than obscured the swish and chatter of the falling raindrops.

Gradually man and wife found some of that mutual consolation in calamity which is the final test of friendship and the enduring stay of love—in a sharing of the burden of their thoughts by simple speech.

"Are there new troubles come to plague young people, Joe, since you and I began life? Must the old people always stand and look on, helpless?"

"I expect we must. We can tell the young ones; but telling isn't teaching, else the world would have grown wise long ago. Ay, ay; it's only the old troubles in new shapes that come to each of us; and sometimes we have to sit by and learn at the youngsters' hands."

His wife tenderly stroked the big hand in her

GOD SENT HIS MESSENGER

lap. "And Ned, Joe; to leave us as he did at the sorest of the trouble—won't he come back soon?" The voice broke on the feeble charge of desertion, and died out piteously in regret.

"I think," Mr. Heyrick answered slowly and carefully, "that we shall never see his face again." He signed towards the dim-lighted window, and lowered his voice to a half whisper as he leaned towards his wife. "I was too blunt and hard with him, Martha. The boy was finer stuff than me. *She* taught me that; she might have saved him. Now? well, he's gone from us; and God forgive me, but it's I that must answer for him if I'm called at the last. I was too hard."

"Follow him, Joe. Take horses to-morrow; follow him and bring him back."

The old squatter held up his right hand and heavily shook his bent head. "He's learned his trade too well, woman—he'll leave no tracks that I could follow. And if I found him? No. He left word for me that meant good-bye."

"He meant no wrong, Joe."

"He has done no wrong—if it was only the guilty that suffered! But he was born with the one sin upon him that never goes unpunished in this world."

"Joe!"

"He's tender-skinned, and he has pity for

helpless things, and he will not," Mr. Heyrick added bitterly, "play Jacob, or bite the hand that feeds him. Oh, his punishment is sure."

Mrs. Heyrick leaned forward and peered curiously at her husband's face in the darkness, keeping still tight hold of his hand. "Joe, you are strange to-night." She leaned back again slowly. "And no wonder, no wonder! No, I can't believe it! Ned gone away, and he spoke no word to me! I can't!"

"There was a change in him when we came back from home." Mr. Heyrick spoke in a measured sadness altogether unusual with him. "I've seen men go that way; turn their faces from their kind and go out — like lepers. I despised them. I called them brutes. I know better now—too late. The child there taught me, though she will never know herself."

Mrs. Heyrick bent forward in a sudden passion of weeping. Her husband leaned above her a moment as though racking his brain for words to comfort her. He found none, and settled back into his chair, merely giving the fingers that held to his own a friendly pressure. For a long time they both listened in silence to the busy frogs and the steady roar of the rain.

Mrs. Heyrick rose to go indoors. She started back with a sob of fear as her toe struck the wisp of paper that lay near the door, causing it to rustle harshly. She smiled wearily though it was dark, as she mechanically lifted the paper, and said weakly, "It's nothing, nothing. I'll sleep to-night;" and she began to unfold the paper absently.

"Ay, you need rest, and "—Mr. Heyrick added with elaborate carelessness—" I'll take the let— the paper, Martha. I dropped it."

He was unpractised in deceit; his wife drew near and scanned his face closely. "You're hiding something from me?" she said.

"Give me the paper, and go to your rest."

"There's more trouble to tell," she said, coming closer still. "Shall I rest, think you, if I don't share it? Come."

"To-morrow, to-morrow."

"This minute." She shook him gently by the shoulders.

"There's trouble, then, from the south as well as the north. My offer for Meadow Flat—has been refused."

"Joe, Joe!—why?"

"I was too late, and the other offered all cash, any way."

"The other—what other?"

"A young man named Creswell—yes, that same."

She reached up and held his face in both her hands. "Old man, it's hard, it's bitter hard; and you'd have kept it from me? See." She kissed him. "Go and sleep; and I must run to my child.—Creswell! There's no luck for us in that land, Joe. And something tells me, as I speak, that there's hope somewhere watching this house." She had grown suddenly almost cheerful as she left him and crept into the dim-lighted room.

Mrs. Heyrick was still unreasonably cheerful after she had bent above the face of the sleeping girl. The face was white even against the white pillow, fragile and sunken, with the look upon it of piteous innocence and utterly confiding helplessness that feeds the pure passion of motherhood and makes strong men afraid. The breath came and went so faintly between the lips—with such a tiny, laboured lift to the indrawing, and such a small, weary sinking at the expiration—that to an anxious, ignorant eye it might have meant that flesh and spirit were fluttering asunder, being tired out in the needful effort to hold the slim body on to life. But the elderly woman touched the moist, cool skin, felt the warm, living fragrance of the hair, and saw how the frail current of the blood had strengthened the colour of the lips; and whispered a host of childish nonsense about health and happiness, and sunny days to come. She was lavish in her promises—as lavish as though she were a fairy godmother, and had the sleeping girl's happiness in omnipotent charge—that the very sweetest and dearest maidenhood that ever God had created and set the sun to shine upon, should not be wasted, and withered, and soured; not if *she* could help it. But last of all, before she lay down at the girl's feet, she cried again bitterly, and poured out her heart in an agony of prayer.

Mr. Heyrick, before he went to bed, watched his crumpled letter turn to glowing flakes in the embers of the sitting-room fire; and as the flakes went black and the last of the busy sparks chased one another headlong through the intricacies of the charred paper and went out, he made a movement of washing his hands and casting something invisible from him. He listened long at the door of the silent sick-room and went to bed, soliloquising sternly upon the incalculable silliness of women.

CHAPTER XV

A Humble Remonstrance

THE world, and all the ages' scour upon it that we call Life, is an open book in which every one who lists may read confirmation in precedent and parable for all his ways and works. Nature importunes us with irrefutable testimony, certifying to the inevitable accuracy of each one of all those fleeting accidents of mood upon mind which we call by the name of ideas and opinions. In the hoarded sayings of the wise every pithy negative is as pithily affirmed in some imperishable fragment of world-wisdom; there are proverbs to suit all tastes, since in the welter that is called Humanity no two of the restless atoms see or think or speak alike upon the single solid ground of Nature out of which they grew.

The country that three weeks before had seemed withered to its marrow was knee-deep everywhere with pasture and herbage of dazzling green; the air was laden with the scent of growing things, and luscious with a mellow, quickening

A HUMBLE REMONSTRANCE

warmth. The little garden-patch of Dinkinbar was populous with tall, rude-growing weeds, that flourished with a barbarian strength and overtopped the shyer, alien plants; grass sprouted thickly to the very edge of the verandah, as if threatening even the earthen floors of the house with an invasion of greenness. The sky had lost its jewelled hardness, and all day huge, stately cloud-flotillas drifted overhead like white-hulled laden merchantmen swimming up-river on a flowing tide.

Susie Thynne had stooped to pluck out some of the weeds that had crowded together in the treasured patch of English violets in the garden. The trespassers were tough-rooted things; she desisted from her work, having made no visible impression on their density, and dragged herself weakly, by clinging to the sill of a window in the bachelors' quarters, to her feet. She peeped into the room; it was empty and in melancholy, mannish disarray. The girl looked down in answer to a tiny greeting; a small kitten was sidling and curvetting along the garden walk in the manner of a charger held on the curb, with her tail arched well forward and showing in her eyes an intensity of mischief and merriment that bordered on paroxysm. She brushed her whiskers serenely on a weed-stem, sat down suddenly, purred her little loudest and stared up at the girl with inscrutable fixity. Susie put out a hand as if the searching eyes disturbed her.

"Weekie, Weekie," she said; "I know now why they worshipped cats and snakes. They feared them, as I fear you, you morsel of innocence."

But Weekie's attention had strayed to the tip of her own tail, which was moving in the grass, and she flung off the role of deity for that of tiger. The girl broke into incontrollable laughter, that spread downward suddenly and shook her till she found herself again holding to the window for support. A fit of sobbing seemed inevitable, but from that she was saved by a return of her interest to Weekie, who was now laid out to spring, as she settled her hind feet beneath her and glared with a fell and drawn intentness at a huge grasshopper that was sunning its bravery of lincoln green in the path.

"Weekie! Oh, let him live!" Susie cried out in agony. It was too late. Before the girl in her weakness could intervene, Weekie had sprung, and a little velvet paw set with a row of tiny blue-black scimitars had swept down the grasshopper as it rose. Weekie wrenched off one of the athletic saw-toothed legs with her teeth and looked up, beaming with pride and purring vociferously. Then she pushed the insect coaxingly with an upturned paw, seeking for an opening to that game of exquisite grace and cruelty on the one part, and tragic helplessness on the other, that is played between a cat and its maimed victim. The challenge was not taken up; the grasshopper was dead, and Weekie strolled away in excellent spirits, working off her exuberance and exercising her alertness in shying at and defending herself from imaginary alarms and attacks from the jungle of weeds.

Susie laid the mangled grasshopper in a little hollow in the fragrant earth, and cried weakly as she pressed down a warm, moist clod over the small dismembered body. She went through the empty house. Blucher, looking unspeakable forlornness and most abject submission and loyalty out of his rich brown eyes, was sitting among the grass in front of the house, and Weekie was "setting" him from the verandah-edge; but as she flung herself recklessly upon him, her wild-beast charge ended in a baby-like hugging of one of his forelegs. Blucher looked down at the kitten in amiable, gratified tolerance.

Susie rubbed one of the dog's ears and said into the other, " Still sorrowing for your mate, doggie? Or do you know as little as I do what it is we've lost?"

Blucher tendered thanks for comfort in his loneliness by giving his peculiar hollow cheer; at the sound of it Weekie disappeared in a panic into the long grass.

The girl went slowly to the stockyard, and the animals followed her, each after the manner of its kind. A running vibration amongst the grass-stalks showed where Weekie was making panther-like rushes; and now and then she would appear for an instant as she leapt up to claw down some winged creature as a living sacrifice to her joy in existence on this splendid forenoon. Blucher kept close at Susie's side, often lifting his rugged eyebrows to gaze up at her in furtive adoration.

The rains had transformed the choking dust of the stockyard into beds of rich and steamy earth, and inside the fences the idle ground was sheeted with a bloom of vivid green, as though the yards were so many forcing-grounds for the spawn of desolation that was come to obliterate the forsaken works of meddlesome humanity. A heap of refuse from the branding-pen was studded thick with creamy-topped, pink-gilled button mushrooms.

Susie stopped to lean wearily against the big post at the corner of the angle that embraced the milking-yard where, on her first morning at Dinkinbar, she had hung back in terrified suspense before she faced the embattled line of the milkers. The moist ground here was thick with the moulded tracks of the cows and calves that had been turned out for the day. As she leaned, Blucher came to stand before her and to look his unutterable sympathy; and Weekie, like a wanderer suddenly restored after years of severance to the bosom of her family, rushed headlong out of the grass, mewing rapturously; she rubbed herself first on the girl's skirts, then wound herself like a figure-dancer mincingly in and out amongst Blucher's shaggy legs. Susie wandered on past the yards and followed up the creek-bank. The dusky plumes of the she-oaks were tipped all over with sprigs of living green where the re-invigorated sap was already building up new leaves and wood.

Crowning a little promontory formed by a sharp curving of the creek below, there stood, wide-armed and shoulder-high above the other trees, a huge old eucalyptian that was ribbed and clamped to the earth with roots like scaly python-folds. The girl sat down on one of these, leaning herself against a rude buttress of the mighty tree-trunk, and looked down the sloping bank towards a little mound of earth. It had been bare and freshly trodden before the rain; but the flooded creek had risen and smoothed it over and ebbed again, leaving river-spoil upon it in the shape of seed. Now, amongst tall grasses there were garlands of bronze-leaved, tendrilled vine, a cluster of blue-bells nodded in the faint, warm breeze, and three tiny sage-green plants were starred with golden immortelles. The small oblong with its vines and flowers glowed like a garden set in pasture-land, and a crowd of butterflies and sheeny-winged creatures had gathered about it. It was Noorna's grave.

Weekie had curled herself down, a pattern of domestic innocence, in the girl's lap; but, having sighted the harvest of living plunder that fluttered about the flowers, she had promptly resumed the part of the slayer by jumping to earth, and, having trimmed her claws in a wisp of bark, she was now drawing near the little mound, showing all the arts of stealth and all the dread fixity of purpose of a hardened man-eater.

The earth and air were singing and astir with sounds and symbols of happy, healthy, new-given life; and yet the girl found in it all a mirror of her melancholy, so surely does Nature speak to us according to the humours that possess our souls. Susie started up so quickly when Weekie's purpose declared itself to her that the green earth swam about her and her knees gave beneath her. She sank down upon the ground and sobbed passionately.

"What kind o' woman's nonsense is this, missy?" Dick the cook, who had spoken, was supporting himself against the tree with one hand, while in the other, tucked against his hip, he held a large soup-ladle. He was looking at the scene beneath him with lofty and bitter contempt, and spoke with a deliberate unkindness that nevertheless was somehow rendered finely considerate by the accent on the last word.

The girl understood perfectly, and looked up tearfully, spreading out both hands, one towards the cook and the other towards the marauding kitten.

"Stop her, Dick!" she sobbed. "Don't let her go — there — and k-k-kill these happy things."

Dick's large and perfect teeth flashed out in his emaciated countenance as he smiled a smile of tired malignity; he hissed three times in a ferocious way, too, which nevertheless brought Weekie flying to his feet, where she rubbed and rolled herself in a frenzy of joy. Dick upbraided the kitten in a few caustic and cutting phrases, and explained, as he clambered down amongst the roots to the girl, where she still sat helpless, that all feelings or demonstrations of gratitude or affection, brute or human, were prompted entirely by a spirit of commercialism. He put his ladle aside, and gently helped the girl to her feet as he continued his discourse.

"And thoughtfulness, Dick," she said humbly, after he had turned away to deliver a few telling sarcasms at the dog, giving her time to dry her eyes. "I suppose that means interested motives, too?"

"That," he said icily, giving her an arm to help her up the bank, "is the strictest business of all. These considerate men"—with bitter emphasis—"is mostly the biggest hypocrites."

"Then," she said solemnly, loosing her hold on the friendly arm as they reached the top of the bank, "I'm afraid it's very little I can do for you, Dick."

The old cook's rage seemed to choke him. He brandished the ladle like a war-club above Weekie, who looked up as if blinded by her rapture, and purred hysterically. "You can come in this minute and take your chicken soup while it's hot," he stormed, "and waste no more of my precious time in running after girls that has no strength and little sense——"

He had thrust the arm peremptorily before her. She cast her weight upon it, and held it to her as they went slowly to the house."

The girl sat long alone before her untasted meal, and was overcome in turn with listlessness and with absurd attacks of an exhausting merriment as she watched the kitten stalking and slaying supposititious enemies amongst the folds of her skirts. At last she rose, and, seeming to quell an impulse to dispose of the food in any but the proper manner, she suddenly carried it boldly to the kitchen, and stood in the open doorway with the tray in her hands.

"I can't, Dick; I'm not hungry," she said plaintively.

The cook bit short a horrible imprecation that he was in the act of discharging, together with some hot ashes from a shovel, upon a few pioneering ants that were seeking to open communications for their main body with his meat safe. With an air of desperate irritation he took the tray from Susie's hands, and set her down before it. He pushed the spoon among her fingers and rapped fiercely on the table. "Would you waste a man's whole morning?" he shouted. But he added almost inaudibly as he touched her hair with the other hand, "Eat, child, eat." Susie attacked her soup obediently.

Presently she paused to watch him. He was spitefully kneading dough. "I've spoiled your holiday, Dick. Why did you not go with the rest of them to the Races?"

Dick pointed sternly with a floury hand to the

soup until the girl humbly returned to it. "Because," he said, and he prolonged the word to a wicked hiss as he resumed his pummelling of the dough, "because I'd have got blazing drunk; that's why."

Any retort upon this would have been either clumsy or cruel. The girl went on demurely with her soup. "There's bread beside you, as well," Dick snapped. She began upon the bread. "That's the holiday you've spoiled," he continued acridly. "You didn't know I made a beast of myself every time I went to town. You never saw me drunk? Well, you never shall. D'you see, missy?" He spoke as if he had, of deliberate malice, robbed her of much innocent enjoyment.

The old man continued to talk as he pounded the dough. At first he made many lurking pauses; but, as the girl continued to sip steadily at her soup and to nibble at her bread, and offered no remark, his voice, after each pause, grew less acid, and his periods less biting, till at last he entered upon a simple, sorrowful recital of his life.

Dick's manner of handling his dough became gentler with his words, as he found his way backward from the muddled darkness of his present to the serener years before the time that his hardest trial had come upon him—before Success had arrived to tempt and betray his better purpose. By the time the dough was divided into loaves and packed neatly into the camp-oven round an empty cocoa-tin in the centre, he gave it the finishing touches quite gently. As he put on the lid and lowered the oven into the bed of ashes, and shovelled ashes on the top, he seemed like a sexton officiating reverently at the burial of his own better parts. He flattened out the top of the ash-heap neatly with his shovel, came over to the girl, and bent above her to look for traces of unfinished food.

She leant back and looked up at him with a tinge of colour in her face that had been wanting for many days. She said nothing; the story of Dick's tangled and broken life invited only the soothing commentary of silence. And yet the girl appeared strangely comforted.

"Your bowl is empty; you didn't pocket any of the bread, maybe?" he said with a touch of his old domineering habit of speech.

She shook her head and smiled. The two looked long and searchingly at one another. In the dulled freshness and the deepened and sobered eyes of the younger face there was some strange affinity, notwithstanding the utter unlikeness, to the older one. It seemed as if the blood-kinship of all human trouble were being proved in a silent mutual confession of the tie of sympathy between these two; in the acknowledgment of a fellow-feeling somewhere between the first sorrows of innocence and the remorse of deliberate profligacy, hardened and irredeemable in its old age.

Dick straightened himself up and looked absently about his kitchen. The upper lip drew in, baring the strong, perfect teeth, and the face took on a look of fleshless rigour.

"Well," he said, soliloquising thinly; "it's the first time this thirty year, you old villain, that you've been a use to anybody—since," he added, anticipating interruption, "you lied to your mother, by letter, so that she might die happy."

"Dick," the girl said gently, "you won't do —do these wild things any more, will you? See how kind you can be when you only think of it! Look how you've comforted me to-day! Listen; I shall write to you, and I shall hear from you that you're always like this——"

"Write?" he thundered, rounding ferociously upon the girl.

"Yes," she faltered. "Didn't you know I was going back—home?"

He turned away and coasted aimlessly about the kitchen. "Oh," he said at last in settled gloom; "I wish to the Lord I'd gone to the

A HUMBLE REMONSTRANCE

Races and let madam stay, as she wanted to. And five months' wages rotting in the Bank too!"

"Dick," the girl cried distractedly, "you hurt me."

He came over and thumped the table with his open palm. "I might as well," he said, looking down at Susie with a kind of desperate complacency, "meddle in other people's business as tell you I'm a rogue and a drunkard. Then you'd see I'm the two ends of an old fool. You're going home," he ended frigidly.

"Yes," she laughed suddenly, then closed her lips and looked up at the ravaged old face as if in doubting wonder at the strange ways by which she was being hurried towards the unbosoming of her pent-up confidences. "I have only brought mischief here," she burst out at last, flinging doubt behind her.

Dick snarled inarticulately, and then retired upon his normal manner of speaking with a new zest, as if to atone for his display of womanishness. "Mischief? my word! And meddling. Look now, this very day you did what twenty couple of workin' bullocks would 'a jibbed at."

The girl looked startled. "What do you mean?"

He slapped the table, and then his own chest. "Kept old Dick from the drink. That's what I mean."

The girl's colour deepened, and she looked down at her folded fingers.

He went on contemptuously, piling up his charges. "And what's more, you've kept another man sober. This young gentleman"—he seemed to spit upon the word as it passed his lips—"this Aplin—I know that breed—he'll be home to-night, and sober at that."

"But what have I done?"

"Spoiled his holiday. You spoiled mine. He'd have had such a pleasant evening—bless you, a whole night!—at the 'Three Bushes,' but for you being here, and weak after your—— And Finlay?"

Dick paused threatfully, but the girl was still intent upon her fingers.

"Perhaps," he went on maliciously, "you can tell me why he has took to washing himself and his clothes?"

Susie shook her head.

"If you'd seen him the other night, then, lying on his face, out in the grass before your window, snivelling—the clumsy colt—at his prayers. And other nonsense."

There was a long silence. Then Susie said,

A HUMBLE REMONSTRANCE

as if steeped in the sense of her own guilt, " I lost Meadow Flat for my uncle, too."

"You did, ay. And you built Cape York, and made all these creeks about here run down hill instead of up. You did that, missy."

He turned away, and began to shovel new ashes on the oven, working almost blithely, as if he had wreaked a just vengeance. "Ah, well," he said with a relish, "we can all go our ways soon, missy, when you knock off at your mischief-making—go the way——"

She threw up her head, and her cheeks flamed brilliantly. But his back was towards her, and he continued quietly after a brief pause—

"—the way that the devil sees fit to drive."

He leaned on his shovel and stared into the fire. "Drink's an awful thing, missy; but there's one worse road to damnation. After all's said and done, if you drink yourself to H—— to death, there's a pub, and there's company at every stage, and you can forget there, and sleep, though the waking's bad and every stage is worse than the one before it. But there's a Bush track to—to the grave, missy, without even a pub on it, or a night's sleep or a day's rest to be had on the way. And the man that starts down that road doesn't turn back—no, not for an angel from heaven."

DINKINBAR

He had spoken quietly and solemnly, but resumed his caustic manner as he laid aside the shovel and said, " They say he will, though, for a woman sometimes; though God Almighty knows I've seen a many go and never a one come back. However "—he added viciously—" these things aren't for the fine folks at home. And I've got to see to these cows. And them that hides can find."

He took down a whip from the wall and went slowly to the door. Susie was bending lower than before above her interwoven fingers. As Dick passed her to go out, a tear fell on one of her blue-veined, wasted wrists. He came back from the door and touched her hair a second time. " Stay, missy, stay," he said, and hurried out.

CHAPTER XVI

A Day's Mustering

THE Dinkinbar pasture sped with astounding haste through the stages of its growth to maturity and fruition. Within a month the green expanse was dimmed and softened by a gauzy purple bloom shed by the nodding seed-tassels; in two months the purple had worn to russet as the silky plumes were ripened into tough and curly wisps, and these in their turn were severed and shaken out by the wind as ripened seeds, each seed pointed like a wasp's sting, and barbed or screw-tailed that it might the better pierce and grip wheresoever it should fall. When the seed fell, the lush and vivid greenness of the stalks had departed, and the grass-tufts were already shot with autumn gold.

At first the surfeit of rich food told upon the famished cattle in a heady exhilaration. They raced about in the intervals of their feeding, calling uncouthly to one another like beggars after a banquet, and often in the stillness of the night there would break up suddenly amid the distant ranges a weird, huge clamour like the bellowing of drunken giants. But with the passing of the short-lived spring and the saddening and strengthening of the pasture into soberer tints and more nourishing and enduring texture the spirits of the herd declined, while their bodies throve amazingly into the normal fat contentment of prosperity.

On a day little more than three months after the breaking up of the drought, the Dinkinbar homestead was astir before the peep of day. Where all the means of husbandry are wholly subject to the naked elements, famine and plenty, want and wealth, are apt to follow hard on one another's heels. Three months ago the weaklings of the Dinkinbar herd had been dying, and many even of the stronger ones had shown their skeletons like symbols of starvation. Then the rain had fallen on the rock-ribbed earth, the whole procession of the fruitful seasons had gone by at the gallop; and now there was to be a mustering round the homestead, a taking tally of gains by the branding of clean-skin calves, and a drafting out of bullocks for the market — a squatter's harvesting.

Already before the daylight Dick's kitchen windows had glowed like beacons in the wide

A DAY'S MUSTERING

waste of darkness, and in the grey dawn there were stirring sounds in the yards, rushing alarums of many hoofs, a jingling of bits and a clang of stirrup-irons, a chink of girth-buckles and a clapping of saddle-flaps, steady "wo-hoas" from the white men, and, overtopping all, as froth simmers on a green sea, the irresponsible, ecstatic gibbering of Moltke the blackboy.

Before the sun had cleared the tree-tops the men had ridden away to their mustering, and Susie Thynne, on whom the convalescent's privilege of a late breakfasting was still enforced, came out to find the house deserted by all but herself and Mrs. Heyrick. The two women were to ride out later to the cattle-camp, three miles from the homestead, to witness the crown and climax of the day's mustering—that finest achievement in peaceful work-a-day horsemanship that is to be seen in the world to-day—the "cutting-out" or drafting of cattle in the open.

It was the first time since her illness that the girl had worn her riding-habit, and the dress that had fitted her so trimly before the troubles of the drought-time had cast their shadows over her, now sat upon her loosely. The sounds of gleeful preparation about the yards and of the subdued sportiveness of the men over their breakfast, that had come to mingle with the girl's early morning lassitude, had served only to point her isolation from the things about her—things in which, since she had declared for a return to England, she was never more to share.

Out of consideration for the girl's weakness, her resolution to quit the Bush, together with other matters, reference to which would have been painful to her, had been passed over in silence. Her going away appeared to be tacitly regarded as an event that was fixed, but as yet undated; and thus, upon the fresh and altered current of life that had come into the station affairs with the rain, she was cast as a visitor and aloof where she had been before an eager participant and a familiar. Every one conspired, in consideration of her unspoken sorrow and of the traces of her illness, to show the cheerfulness that is popularly supposed to be alone adapted to minister to the bodily and spiritual healing of the convalescent. It was finely considerate in intention to leave it to the girl to frame her wishes and voice her perplexity only when returning health and peace of mind should make her equal to the task. But the habit of concealment, like every other habit that, whether owing to determination or the want of it, is persevered in, tended towards fixity, and thus Susie's return towards her lost gaiety grew ever more laggardly.

A DAY'S MUSTERING

Even Mrs. Heyrick—although in her every look, and in her unwonted and cheerful insistence upon a bustling over trifles, she somehow confessed herself hungry for the girl's confidence—joined in the conspiracy of silence, lest Susie's return to health should be retarded by any untoward reference to the things nearest her heart. Except for the one most curious and unexpected outlet for her growing burden of anxiety that had offered itself in the person of the dissolute and ferociously pessimistic cook, Susie, up to the day of mustering, that was to give her lasting release, had been, since the ending of the drought, aloof from those about her and alone with her sorrow.

It was after mid-day before the two women mounted their horses—saddled and brought round by Dick—to ride to the cattle-camp. It was the first time Susie Thynne had been on horseback since the day of Noorna's death, and although her horse—a venerable grey, called Darwin by reason of his wisdom, benevolence, and philosophic serenity of temper—was the most sedate and deliberate of his kind, the very sound of the bit and the cringing of the saddle, the moving strength beneath her and the wide earth around, inclined the girl to a hopefulness she had not known for many a day.

On a high stockyard rail the station cat—Weekie's mother—was dozing and sunning herself, and on the ground a little way off Weekie herself was making furious sorties into the rustling grass towards every point of the compass in turn, from an imaginary citadel as a centre of her manœuvres.

Susie left the beaten track and looked down among the grass to find that the centre of Weekie's operations was represented by a weather-bleached, discarded felt hat.

The women rode for some distance without speaking.

"That was Ned's old hat," the girl said at last in a matter-of-fact way and looking at her horse's ears; "it's strange we never saw it before. I knew it by that hole in the crown, shaped like a Z."

"So did I."

"Where has he gone, Aunt Martha? Did you follow him? have you heard of him? will he come back?"

"I think not, child. We know nothing."

The girl drew a deep breath and looked above her at the open sky and about her at the gold-brown sea of pasturage, and the timbered capes and hills that broke and bounded it.

"It's all so big, and we're so little and helpless," she said at last, in the same level voice. "There seemed so much that I had to tell, and now, when I speak, there's nothing. Tell me, what is it, Aunt Martha? What am I to do?"

"Do whatever's for your happiness, Susie."

The girl shook her head. "You used to comfort me," she said abstractedly; "how is it you cannot now? I want to tell you I'm wicked, and sorry for the way I've used you, and now when I start there's nothing at all to say, and I'm all cold inside. I think you want me to go."

"Sue, Sue!" Mrs. Heyrick said gently;—"if I dared tell you what I wish."

"You see?" the girl answered lightly, turning to her aunt while she helplessly shook her head, holding the tip of her tongue between her small teeth. "I ought to bite it out. Blucher looks at me the way you look now, and understands as you do; but what's the use of talking? I've pulled your house down about your ears, aunty, and I'm trying to run away and leave you amongst the ruins."

"Hush, dearie; it's a better place than when you came, but for the one thing; and the blame for that is mine and your uncle's, if it's any one's."

As on the occasion of her curious exchange of sympathy with Dick, Susie, now that her silence had been again so strangely broken, plunged into an eager recital of her uncommitted sins. Aunt Martha soothingly demolished the girl's vehement self-chargings one by one; and by this roundabout process the two women to some extent repaired their broken intimacy. Once again, and this time more authoritatively, it was brought home to Susie that, although the affairs of Dinkinbar had lain for months in a welter of tragic misunderstanding, yet it was not after all so manifest to others, as she had somehow persuaded herself was the case, that she was wholly, or even mainly, the unwilling cause of the trouble. Rather, in her obstinate blindness, she had been working for good in some mysterious way.

Uncle Joseph's wrath at Creswell's adroitness had, it appeared, been smothered, and even turned to kindness because Susie had been so ill when the news of the loss of Meadow Flat had arrived. Mr. Heyrick, moreover, after gruffly acknowledging to his wife that the calamity "maybe served him right," had, on the night of the rain, after he had heard that Susie's life was to be spared, seemed to repent of his hard bargain with the new-chums, and had given them all their liberty, with the result that Creswell had gone to assume the ownership of Meadow Flat, while the other three had halted and turned back upon their several undesirable ways. And all this—the softening

A DAY'S MUSTERING

of the hard-bitten old squatter, Hulbert's salvation from impending hatterdom, Finlay's vigorous and regular ablutions, and Aplin's restoration to comparative respectability—Mrs. Heyrick on a sudden, rather ramblingly, but with cheerful volubility, ascribed to some subtle influence radiated by the unconscious and self-tormenting Susie.

They had ridden slowly. When Mrs. Heyrick's curious discourse came to an end, Susie pulled up her horse.

"It's quite absurd, Aunt Martha," she said, almost severely. "You've only just thought of all this—made it up as you went along."

Aunt Martha broke out afresh, apologetically this time, and with her motherly quaver—"It's been like the breath in my body, Susie, for weeks, and I daren't speak of it. 'Let the girl go her way,' your uncle said; 'she's come our way to her sorrow. Say nothing till she asks you.' I'd have let you go without a word, my dearie."

The horses pricked up their ears and raised their heads like chargers scenting battle; a faint sound of tumult came down the wind. "It's from the cattle-camp," Mrs. Heyrick said. "Come, they'll be expecting us."

When the two women reached the cattle-camp, the work of cutting-out was well forward, and

DINKINBAR

they drew up in the shade to watch it. Round and beneath a clump of ironbarks in the middle of a plain perhaps a mile across, over a thousand cattle—gathered in from an area as big as that of London—were being loosely held together by mounted men. The tamer part of the business was already done, for about fifty cows with their unbranded calves had been drafted and were being herded in a corner of the plain by Finlay. Down by the creek, Hulbert and Jim Baxter were getting ready for the livelier work of getting out the bullocks, by saddling up the two camp-horses that had been kept fit and fresh for this most momentous of all the duties of a cattle-station.

It is the pride of every cattle-run worth a rap that it owns the best camp-horse in Australia. Dinkinbar owned two such, in the chestnut and the brown that were being saddled now. Your camp-horse is the Raleigh of his kind—warrior and thinker in one—he wastes none of his substance on any of the unessential things that fret his lesser brethren. He must have the dash and fire that comes of high ancestry, and yet he needs a yeoman doggedness; he must be as tractable as water, but of oaken stubbornness to endure; and, at the back of all this rare compound of estimable qualities, he must have that still rarer

A DAY'S MUSTERING

virtue, a brain at once large, liberal, and alert, kindly and cultivable—an equine equivalent of the human intellect that is big but not unwieldy, being quickened with courage and salted with the imperishable salt of humour.

The brown that Hulbert was saddling showed in every point this needful working compromise between the aristocrat and the plebeian. His ears were fine, but a little furry; he was broad-browed and hairy-jawed, but there were slumbering fires behind the bucolic peacefulness of his eyes; he was ribbed like a barrel, but coupled and quartered like a racer; his coat was rough, but there was a silky sheen in it; the legs were shaggy and short-pasterned like a farmer's cob, but they were modelled like a thoroughbred's, and stood wide apart on small neat hoofs as sound as gun-metal. As he felt the girths tighten on his ribs, he turned and nuzzled at the slack of Hulbert's shirt, then set up his head, and eyed the bellowing mob.

Mr. Heyrick on his venerable cob looked, and truly was, like a field-officer leading one small troop of disciplined horsemen against a rabble of barbarians. He had learned, through the fighting of many campaigns such as this, the wisdom of steadiness and a saving of the strength of man and horse till the time was ripe and the rush inevitable; but when the charge was given, it was to be sent home, no matter at what cost of thong and spur. On the Dinkinbar cattle-camp every man was given his place, and kept it.

The two men chosen for the honours of cutting-out pushed their horses in turn into the thick of the mob, chose out a bullock, and edged him gently outward. Several had been thus sent off with little trouble to join the cows and calves, when Hulbert fixed upon one of sterner stuff, a hard-skinned yellow beast, limbed like a stag, a noted rebel and racer of the cattle-camps. The brown horse's eye seemed to deepen in response to a challenge as the yellow bullock set his ears and flung out his tail when he found himself marked for the operation. He came readily enough to the fringe of the mob, but no sooner was he in the open than he wheeled and stretched himself out in a gallop to outrace the horse and double back into the thick of the cattle. But the horse's wide nostril and sunken eye were level with the beast's shoulder, and on the inside. The bullock raced half round the camp, then he planted his stiffened forelegs, bunched himself together as if he had met an invisible wall, faced about within his own length, and the next instant was racing back the way he had come, but faster. The camp-horse was ready; he stopped with the

A DAY'S MUSTERING

bullock, but wheeled the quicker by a trifle. When the return journey was begun, the bullock was going on a wider curve, with the horse's muzzle level with the sharp horns now, and crowding the yellow rebel steadily outward. The shock of the bringing up of horse and man and the wrench of the sudden wheeling seemed more than saddle and sinew could bear; but when it was over Hulbert was saddlefast and sitting lightly. Mrs. Heyrick moaned, overcome with her dread of danger; but Susie looked at the rousing sight with closed lips and dancing eyes. Six times the horse and the bullock thundered past her, and six times there was the sudden shock and swing, and the lightning change of front. At last, bullock, horse, and man tore in a final charge past the tree where the women were. The beast was going with a heavy beaten stride by now, but the horse's lowering eye and open scarlet nostril were steady and sure at the right strategic point on the inside. As they came up level with the women, the three were faced for the drafted mob; then Hulbert unslung his whip, widened his distance from the yellow beast and drew back to the flank, the whip sang above his head, and the cracker burst again and again on the straining yellow flanks. It was the winning stroke; it seemed to cut the last of the invisible obstinate ties that held the bullock to the main mob, and to leave him loose and conquered, to swing off at a free tangent. He went away at a high-stepping trot, making a show of carrying off the honours of war in the defiant set of his ears and his arched and flying tail.

The furious passage and re-passage of horse, man, and beast round and round the mob had set it in commotion, and it was surging outward at many points, and threatening to break away from the horsemen. The cutting-out was suspended, and Mr. Heyrick called up his reserves by roaring to his wife to come and help.

"This is like old times," she said, as she took a short grip of the reins and cantered away, entirely absorbed by the rousing confusion of the camp. Even Darwin, who had been dozing peacefully, woke up and made a perfunctory show of joining in the bustle.

Susie held back the old grey horse, however, and turned him from the camp and towards the creek. Her now customary listlessness had returned poignantly and suddenly upon her after the last meteoric passing of Hulbert, though she had watched him, as he thundered triumphantly by, with a preoccupied and vivid interest.

She withdrew slowly along the creek bank, staring at the ground with an open-eyed but inward look, and she was unreasonably dismayed on looking up—when Darwin, after nickering in a neighbourly way, had stopped of his own accord—to find that she was the object of keen but entirely respectful scrutiny on the part of an elderly stranger, a horseman with a wizened and shrewd but peculiarly peaceful and kindly face. Darwin and the stranger's horse—a mild-eyed, contented old cob—were exchanging civilities by sniffing at each other's noses.

"*Who* are you?" Susie said with a startled vehemence absurdly discordant with the tameness of the situation. "Did you want to see my unc—Mr. Heyrick?" she added with apologetic haste.

"Well, I did, and I didn't," the stranger said in a piping, tired voice; "but I'd sooner disturb a man at his prayers than on the cattle-camp."

The work of cutting-out was again in full swing, and the elderly stranger's face lighted up with a benignant enthusiasm as he watched it. His business, he said, could wait; he had been in the act of unsaddling for dinner, close at hand, when the noise of the camp had reached his ears, and had drawn him to it like the sound of music.

There was a quiet friendliness and a patent sincerity about the stranger that was peculiarly grateful to the girl at that moment. When the old man informed her in a fatherly way that she looked tired, and prescribed rest and a share of his tea, it seemed to Susie the most natural thing in the world, and she submitted to be led away without any misgiving. He helped her down, unhitched the packhorse that he had left tied to a tree by the creek, and in a few moments had unpacked it, and had contrived an impromptu armchair for her out of the packsaddle and his folded tent. Susie tucked herself into it, and was aware of a simmer of enjoyment as she watched the old man extract from his rough but faultlessly neat belongings his ration-bags and billy. As he went about filling the latter, making a fire, and putting on water to boil, he discoursed about himself in a casual way, and so quietly and restfully that every shadow of doubt as to the good faith of her new acquaintance was driven from the girl's mind.

The old man's voice, indeed, was pitched so truly in the right key to dispose the girl to peacefulness that, when he went down to the water's edge to wash and scrub his spare pannikin, although he spoke somewhat louder, his voice began to mingle strangely in the girl's ears with the muttering of the running water near at hand, and her eyes closed quietly for a while. The old man looked slowly round at her, and seemed to

A DAY'S MUSTERING

take all dumb nature about him into his confidence in a single comprehensive wink. When she opened her eyes again, he was standing over the fire with his hand in the tea-bag, waiting for the water to boil, and was silent; but with a demure side glance at her opened eyes he resumed his peaceful discourse.

"Five year, off and on, I followed the gold, and it was always the claim next to mine that struck it, and I watched my old mates make their piles and go all roads from the diggin's, from owning villas and flunkeys in Toorak and seats in Parliament, to dyin' of drink in opium dens or dry gullies, and every man of 'em, by Jimmy, full of a ragin' discontent. I was broke on the Shotover—that's in New Zealand—and of the three of us mates there, one perished in the snowy ranges, and the other's 'doing time,' as I call it, in the ministry of this blessed country to-day, and, by Crumbs, here am I, old Jerry Walker, goin' to make the tea for me and you." He made it with reverent care, stirred it with a stick, and put away the tea-bag in its own corner of the pack.

"I took to shepherding in rangy, starvation country in New South Wales, and one day a bandicoot, makin' a start to scamper from me, sent a loose stone hopping to my very feet. I picked it up; it was like a clinker, and heavy, and sort of rich-looking. 'Silver, may be, Jerry,' I says to myself, and pockets it. But when I comes to camp, there was a big gohanna-lizard, like a young alligator, by Jimmy, fossikin' among my rations, and, says I, 'Silver be—be jiggered; you're not born to be rich, Jerry,' and I lets fly with the clinker at the gohanna's head; and more betoken I hit him, too, and finished him with a stick, and baked his tail for supper; and there"—touching an ancient belt that he wore—"is his skin.

"Well, ten year in and out I broke, with the help of these two hands and this old sun-dried head, all the twelve commandments except the one about murder, and I only stopped short of that because the wife I'd married saved me the trouble by shifting into another man's camp. That was a black night, miss, and I—I was upset, by Jimmy I was. But I found better company amongst the birds and beasts and the stars of a night. I'd done with men from that, and women—and towns. I took to droving, and I piled up enough, bit by bit, to start a run of my own, in the outside parts, out there"—he pointed to the north.

By this time he had set a pannikin of tea beside the girl, with neatly cut slices of damper. "One night on the roads," he continued, "when

A DAY'S MUSTERING

I was waiting to go on the morning watch, I read in a newspaper that they had found the biggest silver mines in the world at a place called Broken Hill, in New South Wales. The clinker that the bandicoot kicked at me and that I shied at the gohanna, that was from the cap of the biggest of the lodes. I was upset that time too, miss—by Jimmy I was. I looked above me, and, by Crumbs, but the stars were driving across the sky like sparks from a fire—they were that. But the stars were steady again when I went on watch. From that time I was the contentedest man in Australia. It was the kind of thing, you see, coming up out of a man's past to show him what he's lost. If he's done with the things that people break their hearts over, it fixes him safe in his own ways; if he hasn't, it sours him, or sends him back again to drive along with the rest, or maybe it kills him."

Susie had settled down to listen with a curious intentness, and was holding her empty pannikin between her finger-tips, with her elbows resting on her pack-saddle. As the old man turned to her quickly after the last words, she held the pannikin out to him for more tea.

"There's things worse to lose than gold or silver, young lady," he said slowly, as he returned the re-filled tin to her. "When I was ready

DINKINBAR

to start my bit of a cattle-station out there, I wanted a mate that was like to be contenteder in the Bush than anywhere within cooee of the towns and the telegraph wire, somebody that would cover my bones from the dingoes if I died first. And I found him, or he found me. I'd seen him once, only once, and told him to track me up and find me about the long cattle-roads somewhere, or out clear of the telegraph posts, when he had got done with this hurry-scurry business, as he surely would. I saw it in him. He came—he rode into my camp in the dead of night, when I was nosin' my little mob of heifers up and out to make my last start.

"Mind you don't spill that tea, miss. Such a mate as he is! I left him splittin' slabs for the house we're to build. But look there now, if ever I was to growl about anything in this world again, I'd growl at this—by Jimmy I would. Here's the Lord sends me all I want in my old age—a man for a mate—and here's the Lord means to take him away again. It's me that is to bury his bones, unless I can bring the medicine he wants. Look there now, but you're shaking, my girl! We'll talk about something else. By Jimmy, now, but that young fellow on the brown camp-horse is a clinkin' rider."

"Go on," the girl said steadily; "I shan't spill

A DAY'S MUSTERING

my tea. What is the matter with your friend? Your story is very interesting. It's not that that disturbs me; I'm a little weak, that's all. I've been ill."

"Ah! look there now! Well, my mate's like me. He's lost *his* silver mine too, and I'm travelling down-country to find it and dig it up and fetch it to him—in a manner of speaking, of course. He can't forget his loss as I forgot mine—see?"

Susie choked down one of her dangerous laughs. "Do you think you'll find it, and will it make him happy when you bring it?"

"Well," said the old man with a slow smile, "maybe, maybe not. I'm bad at this skirmishing kind of talk. A silver mine—this kind of silver mine—in a manner of speaking, may be in the side of a hill, or it may walk on two feet, or ride o' horseback, the way some cove in the Scriptures went to a mountain because the mountain wouldn't come to him when he whistled for it." The stranger beamed with innocent pride in his imagery.

Susie put a hand to her throat, for the wild laughter had nearly overcome her.

"Something has laid hold of this mate of mine, here—" he spread out a hand vaguely on his chest —"deep down inside of him. There's no doctor's stuff to touch *that*. Steady with the tea now. Shall I go on?"

"Go on."

"Well, see now. If a man's bushed in this country, and stops still, he dies in his tracks; the crows and kites get him. Similar, if he turns his face away from his kind and colour, he must go on or turn back, or rot where he stands. He can go on and be a hatter or a combo, which either of them is—saving your presence—Hell. Or he may stick at the cross-tracks and rot, lie there and *watch himself* rot, mind you, which is worse, by Jimmy it is. That's what my mate's doing. Well, let him turn back, says you. Ay, but it's a steep gullyside that—steep, by Crumbs it is! No man works back up that hill alone; there must be a hand held out to him. *A woman's hand*—a woman of his own——"

"Then he's a—a—he's——" the girl broke in passionately, but the words died on her lips. She was as pale as chalk, and trembled pitiably.

"See now," the old man said quietly, "the words, the wrong ones, won't come to your lips, bless you. He's—— Hark! They're calling you."

Above the turmoil of the cattle-camp rose the voice of Mrs. Heyrick calling wildly for Susie.

"Quick!" she said, sitting upright; "he's who, he's what?"

"He's Ned Singleton."

The old man sent a cooee in answer to Mrs. Heyrick's distracted cries; then he busied himself quietly about Susie, who had subsided gently in a faint, swaying across the pack-saddle. A brown stain was spread over the grey habit, for the pannikin of tea had slipped from her hand.

CHAPTER XVII

Martyrs of Empire

TWO men, having breakfasted, were making ready for their day's work. One, sitting on a log, was putting a fine edge to his axe with a whetstone, the other was tightening the surcingle round a loaded pack-horse.

The younger man laid down his whetstone and watched the elder, as he stood behind the horse's tail and shut one eye to observe if the pack were nicely poised and firm, before tightening up the surcingle to the last hole.

"Jerry," the younger man said in a level, hollow voice, "I wish to the Lord I hadn't told you a word. You'll not go near Dinkinbar, or so much as mention my name to a living soul? So help you God?"

The elder man looked round with transparent sincerity in every feature. "Look here, Ned, me lad, are we two mates, or ain't we?" He pointed to the pack-horse and to another that stood saddled near by. "Take the horses and go yourself if you think I'm going back on my word."

"You know I won't, and I know I'm a pig. But you seem to have got some notion about me. *I'm* all right, I tell you. I'll have every stick of timber for the house split and trimmed before you come back. And you'll go straight to the Lands Office and fix up the lease of the run, and order the things, and—and hurry back, won't you, Jerry? So help you God?"

"So help me Jimmy." The elder man was again entirely absorbed in the fixing of the pack. The younger rose somewhat wearily and yawned and stretched himself as though a day's work were done instead of beginning. Then he took up a filled water-bag and shouldered his axe. The other led up the saddled horse and mounted, and the two looked one another carefully over.

"Well, take care of yourself, me lad," said the elder cheerfully. "I dessay I'll be back in a month," and he rode away without once turning his head.

The younger said "So long," and began to climb slowly up a steep ridge that rose behind the camp. A shaggy, blue-grey dog that was crouched by the smouldering camp-fire sat up and watched the men as they withdrew. After apparently weighing inclination against duty, and deciding for the latter, he slowly followed the axeman up the hill.

It was a true frontiersman's camp that the two men turned away from. One could see it had come to stay, for the tent supports were of heavy saplings. There was a table formed of a single sheet of bark, with a rail on either side for seats, under a bough shelter; another rail, with wire pot-hooks hanging from it, was set up across the fire, and already from the camp to the creek there was a trodden path. The camp was chosen, too, with an eye to future developments. It was pitched upon a level plateau that gave ample space for a score of buildings as large as the one of which an outline was already worked out in ground plan by pegs, and high enough above the running creek to set it beyond the reach of flood.

Across the stream was a wide, scantily-timbered stretch of park-land sloping gently upward towards wooded ridges that rose one beyond the other, deepening with the distance into line upon line of airy and airier blue that tempted the sight to measurement of vastness. Horses, free or in hobbles, strolled and shuffled about knee-deep in the gold-brown pasture, or stood dozing in the shade in pairs, head to tail, so that each might switch the flies from the other's face. The pasturage, too, was speckled in the distance with bright-skinned young cattle, the nucleus of a herd.

It was as peaceful an invasion of new territory in the name of industry as could be ; and the wise men who, with no intention of making the experiment in person, exhort the younger generation to rid themselves of this palsy of aimless striving that is the sickness of our time by a return to Nature and a patriarchal simplicity, would have pointed out as warrant of their exhortation these two pioneers and their bloodless conquest of this Arcadia.

Ned Singleton made his way slowly, axe on shoulder and dog at heel, to the top of the ridge that rose behind the camp on the slope. The air was sweetened by the breath of the scented gums, and the summit was pillared by the ash-grey boles, as straight as gun-barrels, of a multitude of pines, and plumed by their feathery, dusky tops. Here and there a tree had been already felled, and lay full length upon the ground, bleeding amber-coloured tears at the butt and from the severed stump, and with a raffle of lopped branches about its head. Up here the air was full of a sunny fragrance that was at once vivid with a resinous tang and sad with a peculiar haunting sweetness from the dead branches, a sweetness that bespoke the active fermentation which is the first token of decay.

The axeman chose a tree already marked for sacrifice, made a rough calculation as to how the disposal of the limbs inclined it to fall, and went to work accordingly by swinging the axe wide and free, and burying its head with a downward cut and a resounding thud deep in the weathered bark. The second blow, a horizontal one, sent the loosened chip spinning in the air, and showed in the cut a crescent of the clean naked wood. A few more downward strokes bared a wider segment of the wood, and two cross-cuts cleaned out the growing wound. Soon the juicy sap-wood was bitten through, and twenty tender curves, the patient records of twenty seasons' growth, were showing in the stump. When the gap had grown till a third of the tree was cut through, the axeman, shifting his grip on the handle, but not his position, fell to work upon the other side, and when the cuts were even he began more cautiously to deepen them and to trim away the corners until a whispering about the bared heart-strings of the tree warned him to be wary. The trunk had sagged a hairsbreadth from the perpendicular, and there it halted, as if braced for a last look round amongst its living mates. One blow on the central straining rib, a mighty crack, a rending groan, and the tall column and its huge framework of branches and foliage toppled and swayed, gathering speed in its descent till the air sang amongst the boughs for the last time, and the tree fell with a crash that shook the solid hill and tore the limbs from their sockets where they met the ground.

Up till now, since leaving the camp, this man, stalwart, capable, firm-knit and silent, might have stood for a pattern of the pioneer, and the wise persons aforesaid—who supplement their incomes by a reviling of the intricacies of an enlightenment that is as the breath of their nostrils—would have gathered about him, if they had chanced to find him at his tree-felling, to sing anthems in praise of the simple happiness of his lot and of their own astuteness in aiding and abetting him to seek and find it. But if they had stayed long enough —which is unlikely, for your philosophic globetrotter is a man of haste—to mark and to divine the cause of the change that came over him as he sat down upon the felled tree-trunk to think, the keynote and triumphantly rounded close of the anthem would have been lacking.

Maybe it is as well. There is little record now in the story of our race of the first few batches of settlers that rotted of scurvy or were scalped or starved or frozen over-sea that the luscious earth of Virginia and the cod-banks and the strip of hungry coastline away to the north o. it might be won as a heritage for the Anglo-Saxon. Sea-robbers and home-keeping speculators, with great Elizabeth at their head, reap in our history the glory of founding the Republic and the Dominion of to-day. And rightly. If it had been our habit to glorify the Martyrs of Empire—even though it is true that they outnumber the Makers by twenty to one—it would not be ours to boast that the dawn is cursed to-day in English all round the world unceasingly. In like manner, if some young Homer were to rise and sing of the warped and withered lives of English men and women now—of the University men that are grain-growing in the Canadian North-West; of the deluded clerks and counter-jumpers that have embarked in honey, fruit, or poultry in New Zealand; of the sons of gentlemen that have gone and are going to scatteration in Australia over wine, women, cattle, and quartz-reefs—God forbid! Let the Laureate of our colonial wastrels only rise and sing; and our Colonies, being docked of the home supply of fancy-fed inexperience, will depart from us at once and for evermore. Let us cling to our national ideals, and let good fortune be the gauge of merit. Let us build no monuments to unsuccess.

The ways of that blind, inexorable abstraction called Providence, when it sets about the business of peopling the waste areas of the world, are the same, no doubt, as those pursued by it in places where the tare-infested crop called civilisation has been sown and garnered through many seasons of the life of man. It is certain, at all events, that Providence is just as catholic in the wilderness as in the town as to the choice of instruments to work to its appointed ends; and it is just as sure in the one as in the other that the ill-adapted will, with sublime indifference to personal feelings, be broken on some invisible knee and cast upon the refuse-heap of the unfit.

The common fate of the pioneer is to sow that others may reap; it is a ruling of Providence that the bulk of the men who force the idle acres into fruitfulness must stand aside to see the reward of their labour given into other hands. It would seem, in the race for the successful occupation of new lands, that the stronger must go to the wall and the laggard win.

Your pioneer, in order that he may endure in his isolation until the slow-creeping tide of settlement shall overtake him, must be re-fashioned to suit the needs of his new conditions; and if, as is likely enough, he is a man of spirit in whom the traditions of his kith and kind are stubborn and unyielding, he is apt to be broken in the remaking.

So long as the axeman on the pine-ridge swung his axe and sent the fragrant chips flying, he fitted aptly into the picture of frontier life of the unadventurous order that was round about him. It was when he sat down upon the felled treetrunk, hunched up, with his hands drooping between his knees and his whole face and figure bespeaking a vague, distressful weariness, that he became at once wholly ill-assorted with his surroundings.

Bim, the cattle dog, when the tree groaned and tottered, had removed himself with a timely caution, born of past escapes, well beyond reach of danger. When the pine had thundered down, he darted in to make an examination of the wreckage of limbs on the chance of finding a stray 'possum. Then he came and sat before his master to show in his gold-brown eyes all the dumb depths of his devoted ignorance and, as only brutes can show to certain of the bitter moods of men, a sympathy as deep as sorrow.

"You incurable idiot!" Ned Singleton said, with a discordant attempt at playfulness; "you know as well as I do that 'possums don't live in pine trees."

The dog drooped his ears to their lowest, and

gazed his gratitude with an intensity that was almost tragic. The man suddenly lowered his head and brought his clenched fists to his temples with an anguished exclamation. " What is it ? " he said many times in desperate whispers. " I must think it all out, and act—do something," he said resolutely at last, lifting his head and setting his beard firmly between his knuckles.

The man who sits down idle-handed beside his work to think the matter out is in a bad way, and the way is doubly dangerous when the work at his elbow needs strong hands and a sound body for its execution. Ned Singleton, as he sat there on the fresh-hewn pine-butt with his chin in his hands, staring intensely and seeing nothing, was nowise singular, but only one of ten thousand other Englishmen scattered about the lonely outposts of the Empire, some of whom, the clock round, are always doing much the same thing in much the same way, and to similar ends.

They are the men who have become strangers to the old, yet cannot take on with the new, and are halted in a muddlesome midway of lunar, airless desolation between the two. They are the Rip van Winkles of the world, the hatters of Australia, the South Sea beachcombers, the scrudds of a lonely corner nearer home. Where his fellows abound, the lazy, shy, unsteadfast, or too fine-spun man may suffer spiritual divorce from his fellows, and may turn laggard in life's race because it is not worth the running, may abandon effort because of the seeming hollowness of all achievement, and may yet be merely ineffectual and comparatively sane of mind and sound of body; these become the songless poets and dumb orators, the barren Crichtons and causeless cranks of civilisation. But that drying up of the marrow of life, that spiritual leprosy of inanition, that wasting of the tissues which no bodily food can arrest, that canker beyond the reach of drugs or scalpel which doctors call, for want of a vaguer term, *pernicious anæmia*, is to be found in its finest perfection of cruelty when its prime contributing cause is the naked solitude of the wilds.

With the riding away of his mate, the last tie that held Ned Singleton from descent into a gulf of creeping madness that had yawned beneath him these many weeks, seemed to have been severed. The man who is touched with the finger of solitude is as firm in the grip of unreal horrors as a nightmare-ridden sleeper. This one sat like a tired horse in a leaden sloth of body and limb; but in his head there was an impetuous and unnatural hurry, as though an engine in his brain had lost its fly-wheel. And yet there was a fell and agonising clearness of introspection. His thoughts, each one clean-cut and lucent, like crystal in the sun, flung his attention, with a dire inconsequence, forth and back from heart to rim of life, and back and forth again. The irrecoverable past stood in one instant stark and clear before him; in the next he felt a famished, boyish craving for the sights and sounds of tea-time on summer afternoons at home—thrushes on the green lawn, the sly song of the kettle, the clean savour of muffins. He lived all his life again in a flash, saw himself go his way, taking as little heed of his direction as water takes in running to the sea, until his road forked where a taut wire sang overhead; he looked up and listened, but there was only the featureless sky above him, and he could think of nothing but that old trick of his, of watching, as he dived off the spring-board into blue water, how funnily the reflections of his round face, and long, pink foreshortened body would be scattered about the surface of the sea before he crashed into it.

His eyes closed at last, his chin sank, and as the hands slipped up and backward the fingers pushed the hat forward till the neck and base of the skull were bare to the torrid sunlight.

He was awakened out of stupor to the conviction that a bar of hot iron had been passed

through his head and roared at his temples.
Nothing else could account for the pain at the
back of his eyes. He was on hands and knees
and the earth and trees were heaving and boiling
madly and about. The only steady things were
the innumerable trunks and splashes of mar-
velously vivid colour that seemed to cage him
in like a netted cat. He was on the very verge
of insanity.

This real danger brought him to his feet and he
swayed and stumbled down the slope retreating
great, to keep his balance for the ground seemed
to heave and dip around him. As he went however the worst of the madness disappeared, the pain in
his forehead had the trees stood still, the ground
grew firm and steady, a strange twilight was tempered
to a most wonderful twilight, a mute and vast serenity such as falls about us in peaceful dreaming.
Something of unnaturalness had gone out into this
unearthly spacious quiet and was become a part of
itself and he watched himself with a dispassionate
curiosity as he fumbled in a saddlebag for his six-
shooter. Yet it was with a himself and with his
own private senses that he felt the warm pistol-
muzzle against his right temple; and when he
heard a faint creaking in the lock as the hammer
lifted he felt a mild and not unpleasant wonder
as to what was to happen after he had pulled

sores, whereat the flies were busy, all cried aloud of a body long given over to uncleanliness; the mazy confusion of lines and furrows about the ochre-coloured face could not be read, when found in company with such a pair of eyes, but as the record of a career of irredeemable vagrancy.

Singleton sat propped upon his hands, and could think of no word to say as he faced his weird, unceremonious visitor. In spite of a gripping pain at the base of his skull, and a sense of nakedness about the top of his head as though there was no covering to his brain, his wits were keenly alive, and he noted the stranger's every feature with a minute and eager faithfulness. He knew the old man from chance descriptions to be a fellow-pioneer who lived beyond the western ranges, amongst a horde of blacks, in brutish squalor, the life of an outcast white man, or combo. He was wondering, with something of the impersonal and humorous wonder of prostration, if fate could by any chance have any yet bitterer humiliation in store for him than to confront him at this moment of supreme degradation with such a spectacle. He had taken away his life, because solitude had made it insupportable; it had been given back to him that he might see what it meant to grow old in the only companionship available for him now. It seemed to him that once again the wire buzzed overhead, and that he stood at the parting of the two ways that lay open to him as an outcast of the Basalt Country, and saw now to the uttermost end of that one marked "Comboism," even as he had before seen to the ends of that other marked "Hatterdom," and on seeing it had put a pistol to his head.

The visitor's silence endured until he had laboriously lighted his pipe, and had filled the tent with a suffocating quality of tobacco smoke. Singleton found himself contending with a hysterical impulse to relieve the tension of his feelings by shouting "Yahoo!" in the old man's face.

At last the visitor spoke, with a dry and stumbling utterance. "Seen a red bull your way, branded H in circle near rump, my brand off ribs?" he said, eyeing Singleton at last through the haze of smoke.

"No."

"Nor a bumble-footed, brown blood stallion, wall-eyed, got a half-ha'p'ny punched out er the near ear, my brand off shoulder, and a kind of saucepan on the near one?"

Singleton shook his head. After all, he noticed, the sound of a human voice and the simple livestock jargon were strangely and suddenly welcome. The visitor swore a long and frightful oath, entirely harmonious with his appearance.

"By the way, what is your brand, and who—my name's Singleton."

The stone-grey eyes looked full into Singleton's this time, and there was an odd twitching amongst the wrinkles about them. "I beg your pardon," the stranger said in a new voice that accentuated his wildness; "I'm Desmond of Moona, over there." He nodded towards the west.

Singleton stared. He had heard of this neighbour hitherto, under the guise of an improper nickname only; now his memory was busy. "The Irish Desmonds?" he almost shouted.

The graceless tatterdemalion sniggered, spat, and swore a blood-curdling oath; but when he said "There are no others—except impostors," it was a Lear of the Back-blocks that spoke.

It was the young man's turn now to look away; the deadlights in the old combo's face had become luminous and piercing. "I potted my first rabbit, sitting," Singleton said, with his eyes on the revolver, "from behind a stone fence, on Taramoona, in Connemara, O'Neil Desmond's place."

The words "my brother" came faintly on a half sob that followed another fusillade of blasphemy.

Both men stared at the revolver as it lay by Singleton's outspread fingers in the sand. A huge stock-whip was looped on Desmond's shoulder; he presently reached forth the whip-handle, and with it drew the revolver over to him. He carefully punched out the six loaded cartridges into the palm of one of his withered hands, swearing again frightfully when he found one of them jammed slightly. He held this out with the butt towards Singleton. The cap was dinted with a fresh and bright depression, showing where the hammer had struck ineffectually upon it.

Singleton's gaze flitted guiltily to and fro, but always returned to the grey eyes, now keen and steady behind the tell-tale cartridge; he pressed a hand on the top of his head, but he stammered out, "I fired at — at a d-d-dingo. Been worrying at the ration-bags."

"You're a —— liar," Desmond said, with emphatic conviction.

"I'd a touch of the s-sun."

"Ah"—Desmond was re-filling the chambers again—"so had I, once. My —— gun missed fire too. Wish to Christ it'd gone off." He faced round and emptied the revolver into a tree-butt about twenty yards away. Not one cartridge missed fire; all the bullets slapped into the tree within a space no bigger than a saucer; sounds of snorting and a clanging of bells came up from the creek below, telling of a wild but brief stampede amongst the horses.

"Got any more cartridges?" Desmond asked, wheeling ferociously upon Singleton. "Out with the —— lot."

Singleton rummaged in a saddle-bag, and humbly handed out a half-filled box marked "Eley Brothers." These Desmond put inside his shirt. "Where's that —— old crow of a mate of yours—oh, *I* know Jerry Walker."

"Back in a month; left this morning."

"Oh. And you were for making crows'-meat of yourself soon's his back was turned. It's a —— fine country, this." Desmond left the tent, and took a Bushman's observation of the sun. "It's noon," he said; "boil the billy. This is my camp, young fellow, till I give further orders."

Singleton crept out, light-headed still, and did as he was told. That his horror of repugnance toward this living embodiment of all that was disreputable in man should have been so swiftly transformed, through the random striking of a common note of memory, into a healing sense of comfort, till he found himself clinging for his very life with a long unstirred hopefulness re-awakened in him, put him beyond the limits of amazement, and set him in that passive and busy concentration upon necessary trifles through which alone contentment is attained and the war with circumstance conducted to a successful issue. The two men ate their mid-day meal almost in silence; Desmond made occasional inquiries, studded with rich oaths, as to the founding and progress of the new station, and Singleton answered them in monosyllables. In the afternoon they went up to the pine-ridge; the younger man was too weak for work, and he sat in the shade while the elder gave practical illustration of the art of log-splitting. In this manner they founded a fellowship on present and immediate things, and by unnamed consent left it to the night before they started upon the more intricate enterprise of an attempt at exchange of confidence.

When they had supped and it had grown dark, they still sat long, staring in silence into the crimson embers of the camp-fire. Somewhere on the black shoulder of the ridge a wide-throated bird communed with the night by calling solemnly, with tragic inappropriateness, " Hot pork, hot pork"; the hasty " cheep-cheep" of a locust would cause the ear to jump and then strain, dreading unearthly alarms; the hollow tapping of the horse-bells, near and far, seemed to deepen rather than to break the huge silence of the earth.

Low down in the north-western heaven a few

stars glowed in a perfect arc. Desmond followed the radiant curve with a knotty forefinger, and pulled sternly at his pipe till in the furnace-light of the tobacco his face showed dusky crimson. "God help us," he said, without an oath, " it's the Great Bear; the stars that shine on Connemara." And at that the two men became as garrulous as schoolboys.

CHAPTER XVIII

At the Cross-Roads Again

TEN days had gone by in the Pioneers' camp. Desmond was still a visitor, and the two men who had thus been flung together in a far corner of the earth had acted and re-acted curiously upon one another.

The random revival of a common tradition served to cast them into a sudden unity; it was a meeting of extremes, of the promise and the fulfilment of two careers cut off from their native surroundings and running on the lines of least resistance to strange ends—a study in the first and the finished product of the lives wasted in the process of reclamation of new lands from savagery.

The consciousness in each of the other's state was fragmentary and vague, and they drew towards such a measure of mutual esteem and understanding as was possible to them by a plentiful redundancy and indirectness of speech; any conscious attempts at frankness invariably caused in Desmond a return of his look of dumb, irreclaimable barbarity. Left to himself, or encouraged in his garrulity by blunt and apparently unheeding response on Singleton's part, the old man would utter, as he strove with rusty speech to follow his re-awakened memories, uncouth fragments of self-revelation, warning, and vague regret. But it was the outward manifestations of Desmond's attempts to raise the ghost of his lost respectability that did the most service in turning Singleton's loathing of him, first to tolerance, and later to a sorrowful liking. To see Desmond toilsomely combing out the knots in his beard, while he chirped in his withered voice of holiday pranks on the craggy hillsides of Connemara five-and-forty years ago, was a sight to make angels weep. And his spasmodic and misty striving after tidiness and decorum in dress and habits was so pathetic an invocation to repentance for wasted years, and so eloquent a plea for the saving strength of opportunity, that it worked in Singleton first a rage of pity, and then a dread conviction that the old age of unspeakable desolation toward which he himself was drifting blindfold had risen up before him as a warning. Time and again, till his better purpose was poignantly re-awakened, across a gulf of years he was confronted with this apparition.

AT THE CROSS-ROADS AGAIN

It was a strange companionship that grew out of this fortuitous meeting of two men, one of them at the beginning, the other near the end, of a life of alienation from their kind and colour. When or how it was to end Singleton dared not think, and the question of Desmond's departure was shunned by both alike from motives, it seemed, precisely similar and wholly opposite. As they were, they dwelt in an isolation as complete as though they had been cast together upon a desert island. It was when the question of their future relations came, always in a roundabout way, to be approached, that Singleton was made aware that the tie between them was slender and dangerous. To sever it meant that he was to be given over to that loneliness which he knew to be unbearable—in the light of latter days he knew now that he would either end it with his own hand, or look on in a cold horror while the fountain of his life dried up. To extend his familiarity with Desmond, on the other hand, was to take up the burden of life again, but with his face turned once and for all from his own people.

The elder man was too hardened a backslider, too long and deeply sunken in his vagabondage, to serve as counsellor to the younger man; he stood merely as a warning and a symbol of sloth. The remorse that was stirred in him was true, but transient; in a few days it lost its keenness, and the rooted preference of long habit for the squalor of his combo life began to reassert itself. The change of temper was manifested with the same ferocious uncouthness that had marked the clumsy and circuitous display of his repentance. Paroxysms of senseless wrath at a horse or a beast, or at inanimate things, had been common with him from the first, and, as the old man's rage lashed him into exhaustion, Singleton would look on in wretched sympathy—he had found more than the beginning of this distemper in himself. Then, later, when the longing for a return to his settled habits began to assert itself imperiously, Desmond sought to justify his "going back on his —— civilisation," as he called it, by a barbarian and relentless sophistry that was the very anarchy of self-righteousness.

On this, the tenth morning after his arrival, he had brought matters to such a pass that Singleton had left the old man in camp, avowedly to ride round and put back the cattle, but really to suffer in that agony of irresolution which the man who is untuned to his circumstances calls "thinking the matter out."

Desmond, with appalling frankness, had for the first time plunged into a precise description of his domestic arrangements at Moona, which he declared must by now, owing to his protracted absence, be in a state of lamentable disorganisation.

What Singleton heard and saw in Desmond's ferocious glee at the prospect of a reunion with his household was the old age of lust—the reality of the poet's dream of a life given over to lotus-eating.

When the old reprobate, sitting on the ground and hugging his knees, let his recital run on to a ribald exhortation to his hearer to come away with him and learn how to live the only life that, after all, was open to a gentleman—"Yes, by — a gentleman"—who had the misfortune to find himself alone in the Back-blocks, Singleton, seizing bridle and saddle, said he would be back in an hour, and fled.

He caught and saddled a horse by the creek, and followed the stream upward as far as there were any signs of cattle-tracks; then he struck out to the west, across the rich, open country. For a while he was absorbed in the work of watching for tracks, and of following them outward to see if the cattle were settling down contentedly in their new pastures. There was peace and abundance everywhere. He was in the tropics, and it was late summer; yet on this high table-land the air, though blood-warm, was buoyant and clear. His course led him westward through the sunny pasture till he was beyond the furthest cattle-tracks, and perhaps three miles from home. Here he was at the beginning of the tract of broken country that lay between him and Moona, and he turned and rode to the south. On the left he looked across the rich spread of his own territory, clothed in ripe pasture, and away down a broad vista of the black-boled, grey-leaved ironbarks he saw where a little mob of cattle was dozing in the shade. On the right, the ground sloped sharply upward into a wilderness of hills, waterless, stony, and crowded with lean, harsh-coloured scrub that in its dour solemnity seemed to scowl upon the broad face of the pasture-land.

As Singleton coasted along the edges of the arid foot-hills, he pulled his horse up suddenly, and stared for an instant amazed at a single line of hoof-prints in the bare ground—the tracks of a ridden horse, clearly, by their depth and evenness. The next moment he looked vaguely above and about him.

"I forgot," he said, addressing the dog, who had withdrawn to a patch of shade, where he sat and panted luxuriously with half-closed eyes; "it's Desmond's track, where he rode into my life; and that's the way"—he nodded sideways toward the wilderness of scrub—"that I can ride out of it, into his. To the west, savagery; to the east, solitude, for good old Jerry's neither the sort nor the sex to make company, even though there's two of us. To the south? Ah, that road's closed for one reason and another—permanently. Let's spin a ha'p'ny at the cross-roads, shall we, Bimulus?"

He rode on along the foot of the desolate, scrubby hills. The border-line between the pasture-land to his left and the wilderness of the ranges was sharply drawn. At one moment the horse would be knee-deep in the golden grass, where it curved in a broad bay towards the rising ground; at the next, as he crossed the foot of an arid promontory of the hills, his hoofs were on bare and stony ground, and the harsh leaves of the scrub brushed the horseman's shoulder. The pasture, the live-stock, and all the beginnings of a thriving cattle-station over there by the running creek, stood with Singleton for the path of duty—the road, maybe, in time, to fortune. And the very thought of it appalled him. The dumb madness of the solitude till his mate returned, and, if he survived that, the desperate hopelessness that this wild unrest in him would be ever tamed to that withered, mild content that brooded in the well-nigh vacant mind of good old Jerry Walker, like serene autumn sunshine! He had murdered all his better parts, and their ghosts would dog him to the end. No; where duty lay, there was death also; death by the creeping sickness of inanition —the leprosy of isolation—unless—— He felt his forehead burn in shame when he thought of Desmond's coming, and felt that even the befouled and abandoned combo, arriving at such a moment, and showing even such a faint touch of human fellowship, had been unspeakably welcome.

He pulled up his horse and looked along the line of the scrubby hills where they rose in their dread monotony and silence against the dazzling blue. Up amongst the slopes a bird chattered, and was still again; the notes were shrill and raucous, and seemed to mock pitilessly. Singleton dragged his horse's head angrily till it faced again towards the open grass country, and struck across it at a canter.

For a while mere blackness settled down upon him when he thought of the single and more than desperate alternative that lay open to him as an escape from the horrors of stagnation, by opening up communication across the western ranges with the worse than outlawed Desmond. Then the workman in him was re-awakened for a little by the care of his cattle as he rode in a devious track towards the creek again, following up and inspecting the outlying mobs. It was noon before he reached the water. The horse plunged his head greedily in almost up to the eyes; Bim laid himself out full length in a bubbling shallow and lapped luxuriously. Singleton crossed the narrow, hurrying stream, and, having drunk himself, he threw the reins upon the ground, letting the horse nibble round him, and sat down against a tree-trunk in the shade.

He became deeply engrossed in pelting with little pieces of dry earth a rugged knob of basalt that stood up in the middle of the stream. The point where he had struck the water was about a mile below the camp; the bridle-track that led up to it was a hundred paces off, beyond a low ridge that rose behind him where he sat. Bim had come to sit beside him, and was gazing intently up the ridge, so intently that Singleton turned to follow the dog's look. Nothing was stirring; the slope stared blankly upon him in the flat noonday sun.

"No, there is nothing—nothing—nothing," he said, and with the last word he flicked a pellet of the black earth at the dog. It struck Bim upon the nose, and he dropped his ears and swept his tail as in acknowledgment of a favour received, but relaxed nothing of his extreme vigilance; he even growled and gave the friendly "wuff" that in dog's language signifies something strange, but probably not dangerous.

Singleton stood up and signed threateningly to the dog to get behind him and be still. Then he went up the slope like a sharpshooter, making for a big tree that stood upon the crest and overlooked the hollow beyond. Before he reached it, he turned and shook a fist at the dog by way of caution, and signed to him to lie down. Bim crouched, looking humble and forlorn. Singleton gained the tree, and, taking off his hat, looked stealthily round the trunk so that the broad hollow came slowly into view from its lower end upward. His heart was pounding vehemently, but there was only to be seen the faint line of the bridle-track like a wavy black ribbon laid among the yellow grass along the centre of the little valley, and the trees with their wide-flung, twisted arms and limp, straight-hanging leaves, all staring and shimmering in a blaze of sun. There was nothing more, and Singleton, when the infinitely monotonous picture had unfolded itself to a point opposite his look-out, desisted in his search, laid an arm against the tree, and leaned his forehead upon it. The memory of a morning at Dinkinbar, when in the dim dawn he had watched the little garden patch unroll its wonders beyond the window-ledge, came back to him. It was that morning, he told himself weakly, that had fixed those old, useless home ties upon him, to the destruction of his peace and the ruin of his "colonial career." He hid his eyes in the hollow of his arm, and a sob shook him.

Behind him the dog gave another "wuff," and followed it by a woolly, kindly growl and small whistlings in his nose. Singleton looked round; Bim's shaggy coat was shivering all over with excitement, and the man, in answer to the dog's earnestness, muttered listlessly, "There must be something there," commenced a survey of the valley from the upper end, and passed in review another blazing, shimmering, featureless tract of grass and trees and winding bridle-track. He thought he had seen the whole stretch of the hollow, but, to make sure and to confound the dog's instinct, he thrust his head far round the tree. A few yards had remained hidden, and in that space there lay a bleached log, overarched by three tall saplings. In their shade there was a woman. She was seated on the log, and in her left hand, resting on her knee, she held the bridle of a venerable grey horse, who dozed above her; with her right she was switching uneasily at the grass with a riding-whip.

Singleton, terrified, dragged himself back behind the tree, and sat down. He stared amazed and open-mouthed at the hurrying, eddying water below him, the browsing horse, the broad sweep of yellow pasture where a file of bright-skinned cattle were now drawing in to water, and at the deep blue line of the western hills. He shook his fist furiously at the dog, but the brute crept up to him and lay down between his feet. On hands and knees, Singleton crept round the tree again, and with extreme caution stood up to his full height beside it. . . . Something must have drawn the girl's attention, for, without moving otherwise, she ceased her switching and turned a pale and very solemn face up to him. For an immeasurable time they looked at one another.

On the girl's right there was a small bare space of ground with a blunt cone in its centre. The cone was seething and astir with a multitude of small and very busy creatures; they swarmed about it in an angry rabble, and the disturbance was spreading outward over the bare ground about the eminence.

Singleton broke the strange pause by signalling frantically, and shouting at the full strength

AT THE CROSS-ROADS AGAIN

of his lungs, "Mind the bulldogs, Susie. Jump up, run—to your left, as hard as you can. That's it; now here to me."

The two were forty yards apart. The girl started to her feet with a scream and dropped reins and whip, but did as she was told. As he shouted his last words, Ned Singleton ran to meet her, holding both his hands before him. They ran thus till only two paces separated them; then they pulled up suddenly, and looked shyly at one another. Bim charged down and tore round about and between the two. He subsided when the girl had stooped to notice him, then backed away and sat down to bark rapturously.

When the dog had grown quiet, the silence between the two was drawn out into a pause of wonderful embarrassment.

"Where are these bulldogs?" the girl said at last, and the words rushed out so vehemently to break the transcendent awkwardness of the silence between them and the spell that held their eyes together, that it sounded like a challenge of bad faith and the opening of a quarrel. They both laughed.

"Bulldogs?—bulldog ants, the biggest and wickedest in the country; look!" He pointed down the slope. All the bare earth by the log was seething with them; they swarmed about the place where her feet had rested.

She shuddered. "Do they sting?"

"Like hornets. I'll go to the rescue of Darwin and the whip;" and he ran down the slope. He picked up the whip, and woke the old horse out of a doze by rubbing his ears, then led him up to the girl. She was standing where he had left her, looking frail and tired now, and childishly helpless.

For one instant he hung aloof from her in his wonderment, with a touch of the old loutish awe that had overwhelmed him at his first sight of her in her radiant health of womanhood. But now on this her second miraculous coming out of nowhere into his life, there was a weakness about her and a forlornness that suddenly gave back to him his lost heritage of man's initiative in the affairs of sex.

"You're tired, Susie. You've been ill."

She nodded many times, quickly, looking at the ground beside his feet, and her chin trembled. He led on the horse, and stood beside her.

"Come along," he said, "over the hill and—not far away—to the water." She had taken off her gloves; she slipped a long, very white and thin hand on his bare brown, furry arm, and went with him submissively. "No explanations," he

AT THE CROSS-ROADS AGAIN

went on. "Complete rest—rest and quiet. I understand—noth—everything. I was expecting you. Not the least bit surprised."

He broke branches and laid them by the tree where he had been sitting. She sat down; he took the pannikin from his saddle and brought her water from the creek. She handed back the tin, and looked up at him for a moment as he stood thoughtfully watching the horses make friends together, while he gently slapped his open hand with the bottom of the tin. She moved a little, making room for him on the branches, and he sat down beside her, leaving a clear space between them.

"What did you think when you met them and they told you——? Oh!"

She had tucked in her feet and was leaning against the tree; he was sitting forward with his hands about his knees, and had looked round at her in amaze. "*I* meet anybody?" he said; then he pointed to the blue line of the western hills with his whip-handle. "I came from over there just now."

"But you said you expected me."

"Oh, well, Bim was sure there was some one over there, and I seemed to be looking for you —that's all."

"And you know nothing at all of how I came, or who brought me—or anything?"

He shook his head. "You're here," he said quietly, knitting his hands about his knees again, and staring out towards the hills. "You're here, and there's neither past nor to come. It's just all right, I don't know how, though everything was in such an impossible muddle five minutes ago. Does it seem like that to you?"

"It does," she answered, and looked at the hills too. "Nonsense," she said presently; "this is wasting precious time. Aunt Martha or Jerry will be back soon, and I must tell you——"

The idyll was broken. "Aunt Martha?— Jerry?" he said slowly, scowling at the horizon now. "Then Jerry went to Dinkinbar, and *he* brought you here?" he said glumly.

She made a weak attempt at merriment. "Did you think I came in a fiery chariot, drawn by Darwin there?"

"Jerry went to Dinkinbar?" He set his elbows on his knees and hid his face from her, framing it in his hands and looking at the ground.

"Ned"—she tried to speak comfortably, and came a little closer to him. She had seen that lost look upon his face before he hid it. "Ned."

He would not look up, though she pulled gently at the wrist nearest to her. She gave it another little shake and let it go. She took a deep breath, looked at the hand that hid his face,

AT THE CROSS-ROADS AGAIN

and seemed to be about to talk vehemently and in haste; but instead she let the breath go out in a weak sigh, and, folding her hands in her lap, she sank back wearily against the tree.

"I'm so tired," she said, "and very, very hungry."

He started up and stood above her. "We'll go," he said. "I wish there was some one here to thrash me," he went on ferociously, and turned away towards the horses. He brought them back and tied them to a sapling near by. "Come"—holding out a hand to her.

She looked up without moving. "Where?" she asked languidly.

"To the camp, of course."

"I don't want to go anywhere at all," she said, still looking up impassively at him. "I've come to the end of everything. It's been just one disaster after another since I came to Dinkinbar. No wonder they called me Featherhead at home. I wonder why I didn't go back there. And now I've come on this last perfectly frantic expedition—oh yes, it was my doing, I believe—I don't the least know why—you're only angry, and things are in a more desperate mess than ever."

"*Angry?*"

"Of course, or else why do you go on as you do, and look like—like——"

DINKINBAR

"Like a savage and a brute, then," he said roughly. "Like an outcast—a leper—as I am, as you told me. There, I didn't mean that, Susie."

She sat up, flushed and angry. "Mean what? I told you—told you what?"

"The truth." He was looking down in his clumsy way and rubbing the ground with a foot.

"What truth—where—when?"

"By the water-hole, at Dinkinbar."

"You touchy, sulky bear," she retorted, laughing up at him and shaking her head. "Look at me. Come, what was it?"

He looked down at her. "The night—the night I left."

She laughed delightedly. "You silly, *silly* boy. You do look like the Ned I knew once, though, now." She had laid her head critically to one side. "The night you left, and for ages and ages since, I was ill, and it's all gone—all. I remember something about our first real afternoon tea on Dinkinbar, but nothing since until just the other day."

"And what did they tell you?"

"I was going home, and they said something about you disappearing with some notions of duty and about making a start for yourself, and something about a quarrel with Uncle Joseph, and all that. *I* thought it was inconsiderate of you, to say the least of it, to ride off and leave me in the jaws of death."

"I didn't, Susie, I didn't."

"No, no, I know." She put her hands to her head in a bewildered way.

"We must go," he said firmly; but he began to pace to and fro in front of her as she sat limply, gazing at her idle hands. His eyes travelled continually from the hazy blue line of the hills to the figure of the girl. At last he stopped before her. "Sweekie," he said gently. She looked up quickly at him. "Why did you come?"

She stooped lower still, completely hiding her face from him. "He said—Jerry said—you were—I thought I'd like to see you before I—go away home." She tried to go on, but the words died away in whispers.

"Come along," he said, holding out a hand to her; but she did not see it, and tried to rise without his help. She was cramped and weak, and when half risen she stumbled backward towards the tree with a little moan.

He flung down his whip and caught her, so that her head swayed backward, narrowly missing the tree. For just an instant as she gathered her feet beneath her, the eyes looked up into his; he saw the tired, sweet mouth, the line of little teeth, and felt the weight of the warm, weak body in his arms and her breath in his face and his dour, hard indecision vanished. The next moment she was sobbing heartily on his neck.

"Between old friends, it's allowable," he said as he stroked her hair.

It is an odd thing that, although the solitary traveller finds the path of life so exceeding strait and so closely hedged about on either hand with mystery and horror, yet when two go abreast there is ample room, and much of the horror fades, and much of the mystery is made plain. These two seemed to find everything absurdly simple and satisfactory, though they made it as clear as abundant iteration could that they had merely joined together the broken ends of an old boy-and-girl friendship, and were soon to part.

Soon they were riding slowly towards the camp; half-way there, they met Aunt Martha hurrying towards them. She pulled up her horse while they were still far off, and sat awaiting them. By the time they had drawn near, Mrs. Heyrick seemed to have gathered from a steady contemplation of them that the cruder and plainer elements of the new situation demanded all her housewifely energy, and that the vaguer and subtler things could take care of themselves. Accordingly, she gave Ned a dry, almost blunt,

AT THE CROSS-ROADS AGAIN

and quite conventional greeting, and opened on him at once with stern upbraidings as to the abysmal untidiness of the camp. "And who's the dirty, wild old man we found there in place of you?"

Ned whistled. "I'd forgotten him. It's only a later edition of me as the pioneer, Aunt Martha."

"God forbid," she said earnestly.

"Amen; but what in the world are we going to do with him?"

When they reached the camp, that question was settled, for old Jerry was watching the retreating Desmond as he rode slowly away among the yellow grass beyond the creek.

Singleton drove his own horse half down the slope, and called to the old man again and again; but Desmond would not turn his head or stop. He waved his hand once in a wearyful way, and rode on to the westward.

Singleton looked long after him, and was full of a wild sorrow, a nameless horrible regret, until he turned again and looked up the slope. Jerry was looking down at him; and behind him he could see the women, merry and busy about the bark table, setting out the rough accessories for the mid-day meal.

"The cross-roads again," Singleton said to

himself, and he looked above him, as by long habit, for a singing wire; "but the way back is open now. There, without the grace of God, would I have ridden—or stayed? I do not know."

He came up to old Jerry, and punched him softly in the chest. "You tinker, what about the Lands Office?"

Jerry beamed his most benevolent old smile. "It'll keep, me lad; t'other business was urgent."

12mo, cloth, $1.25

THE MAN WHO WAS GOOD

BY
LEONARD MERRICK

AUTHOR OF
" A Daughter of the Philistiees," " One Man's Views."

"A second success. . . . . An exceptionally able novel."—*Literary Review.*

"Remarkable for its splendid delineation of character, its workmanship and natural arrangement of plot."—*Chicago Daily News.*

"Has distinction of style and character, dramatic force and literary effectiveness."—*Phila. Press.*

"An intensely dramatic story, and written with force and precision."—*New York Times.*

"Mr. Merrick's work is of a very high quality. Is the most masterly of his three books."—*Chicago Tribune.*

"The delicacy of the character sketching has a brilliancy and fasciuation strangely magnetic."—*Minneapolis Tribune.*

"Is a forceful, dramatic and altogether human story of English life."—*Boston Times.*

"Strong story."—*Chicago Record.*

"It is useless to say that so strong, so fierce a book must be written well."—*Chicago Times-Herald.*

NEW YORK
R. F. FENNO & COMPANY

12mo, cloth, $1.25

THE DAGGER AND THE CROSS

BY
JOSEPH HATTON

Author of "By Order of the Czar."

❧ ❧ ❧

"Most dramatic manner..... Deserves to rank well up in current fiction."—*Minneapolis Tribune.*

"Villainy of the deepest die, heroism of the highest sort, beauty wronged and long suffering, virtue finally rewarded, thrills without number."—*St. Louis Globe-Democrat.*

"Clean wholesome story, which should take prominent place in current fiction."—*Chicago Record.*

"Finely conceived and finely written."—*Toledo Blade.*

"This is his masterpiece."—*Buffalo Express.*

"The chief merit is the account of the Plague in Eyam..... It is a true story and Eyam is a real village."—*Boston Journal.*

"Weird and interesting to the point of being absorbing. The only way to get the story is to read it."—*St. Louis Star.*

"Seventeenth century romance steeped in the traditions of the Church and of the times."—*Detroit Journal.*

NEW YORK
R. F. FENNO & COMPANY

www.ingramcontent.com/pod-product-compliance
Lightning Source LLC
Chambersburg PA
CBHW030807230426
43667CB00008B/1100